June 30,

Dear Harr and ———

Having next door neighbors, Marie and I feel very lucky to have you guys so constantly helpful. We both are so very happy to have made our home alongside you at HARBORVIEW.

James Andrew Jim - Jimmy Shanley

MW01250610

A
Plum
Life

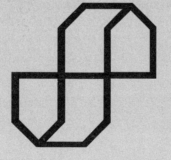

A
Plum
Life

By James A. "Jim" Shanley

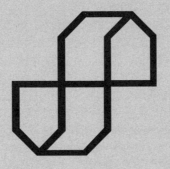

PETER E. RANDALL PUBLISHER
Portsmouth, New Hampshire
2015

James A. "Jim" Shanley is a retired realtor who owned James A. Shanley Corporation and operated twelve real estate offices throughout New Hampshire and Maine. He was born and raised in Portsmouth, New Hampshire, and earned degrees from the Boston University School of Business Administration and the Boston University School of Law. He served in the U.S. Navy and survived metastatic melanoma cancer. He has traveled extensively over the world and continues to live "a plum life" with his wife, Marie, in New Castle, New Hampshire.

© 2015 James A. Shanley
All rights reserved.
ISBN 13: 978-1-937721-23-7
Library of Congress control number: 2015937893

Published by:
Peter E. Randall Publisher
Box 4726
Portsmouth, NH 03802
www.perpublisher.com

Book design by Grace Peirce, www.nhmuse.com

To my wonderful family and friends

Contents

Foreword

The McCaffery-Shanley family has been a part of Portsmouth, New Hampshire, for generations. I first met Jim Shanley when I was a Portsmouth police captain and department historian. Mr. Shanley arrived at the Police Department asking for a photo of his grandfather, James John McCaffery, who had served the Portsmouth Police Department as a police officer for forty-seven years. We talked about his grandfather over the next hour and the impact he had on the community one hundred years before. Since then we have remained friends, exchanging historical stories and a lunch from time to time. When I was promoted to Chief of Police, it was Mr. Shanley who made one of the first phone calls to congratulate me, followed by an order to "do a good job." I relied upon him for advice, mentorship or just a joke when I needed one. He often disguised his "lesson of life" in stories that he or a member of his family had experienced. I am happy that he has written many of these same stories within this book, a book about the McCaffery/Shanley legacy, their place in history, and life in general.

It is said that history repeats itself or at least rhymes. The family understands this as well and has collected and published their stories so that we may learn from them. We also find in these historical accounts, the importance of community service, family love, and working each day to make oneself a better person. I hope you too enjoy the stories.

Dr. David "Lou" Ferland
Portsmouth, New Hampshire, Chief of Police (Ret.)
Professor, Mount Washington College

PART I

ORIGINS AND YOUTH

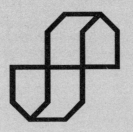

CHAPTER 1

John "Mac" ("Blackjack") McCaffery

I feel it would be best to begin the first chapter with writing the story of John McCaffery, nicknamed "Mac" and later called "Blackjack."

He was born at Portaferry, County Down, Ireland, on November 16, 1830. He left home at fifteen years of age and became a "blood boy" on a British man-of-war. A warning to the reader with a queasy stomach: I am told that "blood boys" were called such because they had to sweep body parts over the sides of the ships while battles were raging. Even though we see magnificent oil paintings of French, Dutch, Spanish, Swedish and Norwegian battleships, with two battleships of that period in full sail—cannons roaring and smoke fumes shooting—they would in fact lash onto each other with hooks and ropes and blast away, causing great damage. Essentially, bodies would be decimated. The duties of the "blood boys" were to clear the deck.

"Black Jack" eventually landed in New York City on his British man-of-war, and family lore is that he jumped ship. Unsuccessful in finding any employment on shore, he concluded to enter the U.S. Navy on September 19, 1846, at Boston, Massachusetts. We have a Navy record that he fought for the United States in the war against Mexico. On February 17, 1847, he was aboard the battleship *Ohio*, which sailed for Veracruz, Mexico. He participated in the siege and capture of that Mexican stronghold and of the celebrated Mexican fortress known as the San Juan de Ulúa.

After the capitulation of Veracruz, the Home Squadron under the command of Commodore Perry then sailed for Tuxpan and captured that city, and later the important port of Alvarado. The *Ohio* was then ordered to New York and thence to Brazil and the Pacific coast, going to Valparaíso, Chile; Callao, Peru; and Mazatlán, on the west coast of Mexico; capturing that city and fortifying it until the close of the war.

In 1849, the *Ohio* was ordered to the Sandwich Islands, where the men were given their first liberty in eighteen months, returning afterwards to San Francisco. Here, young McCaffery was transferred to the battleship *Edith*, which shortly after wrecked in Conception Bay. The crew finally reached San Francisco, where McCaffery's time expired and he was discharged with several hundred dollars in his pocket.

The "gold fever" was then at its height, and "Mac," bent on getting rich, went to the mines and remained there for three years. He then returned to San Francisco without a penny to his name. Finding a merchant ship about to sail for Hong Kong and London, his name was quickly signed to the articles. Ten months later, in 1854, he found himself in New York, where he again joined the Navy, shipping on board the sloop-of-war *Cyane* for three years. At the close of his service in 1857, he was enlisted and served successfully on board the USS *Merrimack* and USS *Roanoke*. He sailed on both ships with Midshipman Carpenter (who later became a rear admiral and coincidentally retired on the same day "Mac" died) and also sailed with Robert Bradford, later a captain.

He was discharged at the Brooklyn Navy Yard and married a Brooklyn lady named Mary Galliger. He became a widower and subsequently married Sarah Jane Langan.

At the outbreak of the Civil War, he once more entered the service of his adopted country, this time in the Revenue Marine and later in the U.S. Coast Survey. On April 22, 1862, he again entered the regular U.S. Navy, shipping on the USS *Dawn*, attached to the North Atlantic Squadron. On August 6, 1863, he was appointed master's mate, and on January 22, 1864, as acting gunner. On January 18, 1866, "Mac" was appointed boatswain and remained in active service until December 20, 1889, when he was retired from a disability. With a long and honorable service, upon retiring he was stationed at the Portsmouth Naval Shipyard.

At some point during his service, Chief Boatswain McCaffery came into notoriety by being charged with the drowning murder of a sailor on his ship. The sailor had been accused of committing a crime and was punished by being "keelhauled." Wikipedia defines keelhauling as:

> [A] form of punishment meted out to sailors at sea. The sailor was tied to a line that looped beneath the vessel, thrown overboard on one side of the ship, and dragged under the ship's keel, either from one side of the ship to the other, or the length of the ship (from bow to stern). As the hull was usually covered in barnacles and other marine growth, if the offender was pulled quickly, keelhauling would typically result in serious cuts, loss of limbs and even decapitation. If the victim was dragged slowly, his weight might lower him sufficiently to miss the barnacles, but this method would frequently result in his drowning. Keelhauling was legally permitted as a punishment in the Dutch Navy. The earliest official mention of keelhauling is a Dutch ordinance of 1560,

and the practice was not formally abolished until 1853. Keelhauling has become strongly associated with pirate lore.

By my family lore, the alleged facts were that the ship's crew divided equally, each with a rope tied to the hands and feet of the accused, who was then thrown over. Upon order, the crew raced to get the sailor to the front of the ship. In this particular case, the accused drowned. If he had survived, it would have proven his exoneration and he would have been released. Since he drowned, Blackjack was indicted for murder, tried at the Portsmouth Naval Shipyard and acquitted.

After his retirement, he settled down in Portsmouth. It is reported he was "very popular." He served one term as alderman from Ward 2 and was very active in the veteran organizations, particularly the Kearsarge Naval Veterans Association and General Gilman Marston Command of the Union Veterans' Union (UVU).

Blackjack's last wife was Alice Linchey, who is buried at Calvary Cemetery in Portsmouth with three of her children. It should be noted that after his death, Alice filed a declaration for a widow's pension "for support of herself and for her four minor children." The declaration stated that he died leaving "The Homestead No 29, Wibird St. Portsmouth, N.H. valued at about $1800 and the furniture therein at $350 and one cow valued at $30."

The U.S. Navy and Portsmouth Naval Shipyard would continue to play an active role in our family in the generations that followed.

Obituary of John "Mac" AKA "Blackjack" McCaffery

From the *Portsmouth Herald*, 30 September, 1897:

Boatswain John McCaffery, U.S.N. retired, died at his home on Wibird Street at 2:38 o'clock this Thursday morning, after a short illness, at the age of sixty-six years, ten months and fourteen days.

Boatswain McCaffery had been in failing health for a year or more, but was able to be about on the streets until a couple of weeks ago, when he was stricken with the malady that ended his useful and honorable career . . .

He leaves a wife, five sons and four daughters, all residents of the city.

CHAPTER 2

Grandparents: James Andrew and Mary Ellen McCaffery

We formally leave "Blackjack" behind as we proceed to the life of my grandfather, James Andrew McCaffery, and his wife, Mary Ellen (Leary) McCaffery.

My grandparents were both born and raised in the area in Portsmouth known as "the Railroad Tracks." This was south of Islington Street. In between Islington Street and Middle Street was an area where many other nationalities lived. Eventually, the "North End" was mainly inhabited by Italian arrivals.

The frank truth of the matter is that, historically, the Irish men were brought over to work in the field and the women to become nannies and cooks. My grandfather was a police officer, and he was determined that his children were not going to be laborers. My grandfather had a career in the Portsmouth Police Department for forty-seven years. He began his service in 1895 and was a patrolman until 1919. He became captain of the night watch (they didn't use the word "chief") when the Republicans controlled Portsmouth politics. When the Democrats were re-elected in 1925, he was put in charge of patrolling the brothels along Marcy Street.

My grandparents fell in love and were married. The children were Frederick J. McCaffery, Margaret McCaffery, and Marie Gertrude McCaffery (my mother). My grandfather bought a lot of land on Wibird Street, and in Portsmouth it is reputed to have been the first sale in the area to an Irish Catholic. Before that time, it was reported that Portsmouth was divided into the "Crick Irish" and the "Yankees" from Middle Street to South Street. He built 279 Wibird Street on the lot, and everyone says he bought it for a week's pay. The family remembers living in the house with no plaster on the inside, just slats. In the basement was a coal fired boiler.

My grandmother and he moved into the house with their son Frederick, daughter Margaret, and my mother, Gertrude. With so many women in the house, my grandfather was a quiet man!

There are so many stories of my grandmother, but one I especially remember is that at the first clap of thunder, she would sit in the hall in her rocking chair with her rosary beads looking out the open front door waiting for the lightning. There was a photograph on the wall of a howling wolf, and I treasure that photograph in my home to this day.

My grandfather obviously loved my grandmother dearly, and underneath it all, they were very excited to have their first grandchild from their daughter, Marie Gertrude McCaffery. As you can see in a picture of me as a baby in the arms of my grandmother, I was her first grandchild, and deeply loved.

One of my earliest memories of my grandfather has to do with the basement bulkhead at 279 Wibird Street. It was a wooden covered entry to the basement. I would constantly pick it up and slam it shut, causing a tremendous bang. I knew my grandfather would come storming out of the house, but he had a row of big bushes, and I would hide behind them. Because of his age, he could never catch me. I now know that he must have thoroughly enjoyed the continuing chase. I lived with him as a little boy from five or six until I joined the United States Navy. When I came out of the Navy, I continued to live with him until I was married.

After all is said and done, the most important thing my grandfather taught me was that integrity and honesty were paramount in the conduct of living a productive and happy life. An example was this: he and I were forever playing checkers, cribbage, and the card game of casino. He would win most of the time, and he would never let me win unless I absolutely won.

Of course, my grandmother, as all the McCaffery-Shanley women, ruled one way or the other. Her children were truly dedicated to her. Their son, my Uncle Freddy, was drafted into the army at the time of World War I. He started his training at Camp Langdon in New Castle. Every evening, he would jump the fence from camp, sneak home, and get his supper at 279. He would sleep in his own bed and then get up very early in the morning so he would be back in time for roll call. He was the nicest uncle. Man alive! He became a machinist at the Portsmouth Naval Shipyard, in a way also continuing the Navy tradition begun by Blackjack.

My grandfather always had a uniform and came home with a big revolver, He put the revolver on the desk I have. Only once did I handle his revolver, and the reaction was such that I never touched it again.

Prostitutes were brought to Portsmouth from Boston in those days by train. The madam would put them in a carriage dressed in their finery while she sat on her dais at the rear. They would be paraded from the train to Market Street and around Market Square before being placed in the various houses of prostitution along Marcy Street. The houses were an open secret protected by the head of the police department for many years.

I never realized what a police officer did until I was a U.S. sailor on shore patrol in the Navy years later.

The following was taken from the *Portsmouth Herald* in late 1940:

> Probably the greatest tribute that can be paid anyone and especially a police officer, for maintenance of law and order, was paid Capt. McCaffery, last evening when a party of sailors from the U.S.S. *Camden*, which is to leave port next Thursday, visited the station in a body to bid "Mac" good-bye. There were over a dozen smiling, good natured sailor boys in the party who in their rough and ready way, showed their appreciation of his friendship to the boys while here and expressed their regret at the parting with the good natured captain.

I was devastated when he died, and I couldn't let him go. I wouldn't go to bed. He was laid in front of the three windows at 279; they had his corpse with all the flowers there. I sat by him all night. Officers would drive by and come into the house one after the other. They were all on patrol or purposely wanted to say goodbye one by one. He was so popular.

We had a wake for my grandmother at the house as well. In my youth, it was the way the Irish had wakes. It was a good excuse for people to get together and drink. When my parents died, we had services at John Farrell Funeral Parlor—with no alcohol—home wakes had disappeared by then.

The Portsmouth Police Department has a large, locked room that contains uniforms, old guns, swords, etc. Because my grandfather served forty-seven years on the police force, I often would go to the desk sergeant and ask him to unlock the room for me. The ambition of Chief Lou Ferland and I was to move these arti- facts to an abandoned building. It was behind the ancient Ports- mouth Public Library, a magnificent architectural gem designed by the famous Colonial-era architect Charles Bulfinch. I had my crew of carpenters, plumbers, electricians and painters examine this three-story building. I was prepared to renovate and move the PPD museum to the first floor, so it could be shown to the community to give pride to the PD for PPD artifacts, but it never worked out.

Obituary of James McCaffery

From the *Portsmouth Herald*, 17 January, 1950:

A veteran of nearly 50 years [sic] service with the Portsmouth police department died today at the age of 81.

James A. McCaffery died this morning at his home at 279 Wibird Street [sic]. He served 47 years on the local police force, one of the longest active police service records in New England

He was appointed to the police department April 2, 1895, one of the first appointments under the police commission system. A former caption of the night watch, McCaffery was acting captain of the night watch at the time of his retirement Jan. 1, 1942.

He was a member of the Church of the Immaculate Conception and of the New Hampshire Police Retirement Association.

A native of Brooklyn, N.Y., he was born Feb. 1, 1868, and had lived here for 70 years.

Survivors include his wife, Mrs. Mary E. McCaffery; two daughters; Mrs. Leo F. Power of Roxbury, Mass., and Mrs. Joseph J. Shanley of Portsmouth; a son, Frederick T. McCaffery of Portsmouth; a sister, Mrs. Mary E. Long of Bath, Me., and a brother, Thomas F. McCaffery of New Castle.

Obituary of Mary Ellen McCaffery

From the *Portsmouth Herald*, March 2, 1955:

Mary Ellen McCaffery, 279 Wibird St., died March 1. Funeral from her late home Fri. morning 8 a.m. High Mass of Requiem at the Church of the Immaculate Conception at 9. Friends invited and may call after 6 p.m. today. Arrangements by John G. Farrell.

CHAPTER 3

Parents

My parents met at a dance.

My father came from Brighton, Massachusetts, in World War I and worked hard at the Governor Fuller Mansion as a groundskeeper before joining the Shattuck Shipyard in Newington building wooden vessels that carried munitions and armaments to the troops battling in Europe. His brother, Al, passed away about that time, at age twenty-six from tuberculosis, when my father was building wooden boats called "Liberty Ships." They were used for taking ammunition and supplies during WWI. Later, he was employed at the Portsmouth Naval Shipyard and worked as a welder during World War II. He was sent to the University of New Hampshire by the federal government during the war to study metallurgy. He had no other formal education, but they did sense his brains. He came from nothing but came to oversee eight hundred other welders building submarines in his career.

After my father came here to the shipyard, he remained close with his family. He was the oldest child in his family, and all of his brothers and sisters were extremely smart. Uncle Paul never married and was an accountant for the City of Boston. Aunt Mary gave me my first radio.

When his mother and father died, the church put all the Shanley kids on the altar. This was the custom back then; all the orphaned kids were lined up and people in the church picked. "Aunt Delia" chose my father, my Aunt Mary, my Uncle Paul and my Uncle Frank. We don't know if Aunt Delia was a blood relative; there was no obvious connection. Aunt Delia helped raise my father, but some of the kids were split up, with some going to relatives and others to church members. The Shanley kids who were adopted retained their Shanley name.

My father also started as a young man cutting the lawns at Governor Fuller's home in Rye, New Hampshire. The Governor married a Catholic and built a beautiful chapel in the back. The home was eventually owned by a real estate mogul who came over from Ireland without a dime.

My mother was a knockout, so a lot of young men tried to inveigle my grandmother to let them marry her, and many of them were educated. My father would come to my mother's house, and he was madly in love. One thing in his favor was that he was Irish, and we were all Irish, but the Yankees from the prominent families were always coming by, too. My mother attracted bees to the honey. In Portsmouth, a lot of people wanted their daughters to marry into the local gentry, but my grandmother was a good judge of character and knew my father. As befit the forever dictatorial nature of the female members of the Shanley tribe, she said to my mother, "You are going to marry Joe Shanley from Brighton." What can I say? The arrangement worked out for me!

Because of age differences and other things, it's hard to really ever know your parents, but one thing sticks out. When I was a teen, there was a real pool parlor nearby, and in my mind, I could really shoot pool. I didn't know anything about my father's background in Brighton, but he was an avid Elk and did massive charity work, holding a lot of positions in that organization.

Apparently, he also shot a lot of pool. I asked him once, "Dad, would you let me shoot some pool at the Elks?" So we went in the cellar there—it was really like a movie set. He racked the table and let me break. Then he ran the table. When all was said and done, he put his pool stick up and I put my stick up and we went home. That was it.

In the house where I grew up, women had the power. The Shanley women ruled the roost. Everyone remembers my mother's method of ruling—she swooned. The women in our house never fought. Each woman had a floor for which they took charge, but my mother ruled over all with her swoons. If anything went wrong on that my mother didn't like, she would fall into her chair. At four o'clock, my father and Uncle Freddy would come home from the Navy Yard starving. When I was home and my father came through the front door, if he caught my mother having one of her performances, he would say, "Please go upstairs and talk to your mother." I'd take my mother's hand and convince her to come downstairs for dinner. I loved her, and my children sure did, too. If I was in town and not traveling, I had to be home by four in the afternoon. Growing up at 279, we shared all our meals at night.

My mother was obviously proud of me but never let on. My sisters tell me now she drove them crazy behind my back by doting on me in secret. She would watch her bank CDs like a hawk and have me bring them back and forth; they were like gold to her. She knew I knew a lot about banking finances.

When my father came home from the Navy Yard during World War II, just before I went to work over there, he had a chair in the living room. When I'd come home, I'd sit next to him on the couch and we would chat and the enjoy the news. He'd go upstairs and my mother would be swooning again. He would unburden himself to me about some ungodly thing. He was too old to go into the service, so his contribution was working six days a week at the Navy Yard.

A lot of people in Portsmouth remember the horrible loss of the nuclear submarine the USS *Thresher* in 1963. What people may have forgotten is the earlier sinking, in 1939, of the USS *Squalus*, another submarine, also built at the Portsmouth Naval Shipyard. My dad was working at the yard when the *Squalus* had an explosion at sea and sank near the Isles of Shoals. Unlike the *Thresher*, the *Squalus* sank in shallow water and the Navy discovered there were still men alive inside her. It was a dramatic event—communicating with the trapped men, figuring out how to rescue them. It was horrible, but fascinating. I think over half the crew ended up surviving, but the loss of life was still awful. After they rescued the crew, they had to figure out how to reclaim the sub, and finally did. It was towed from the Isles of Shoals up the Piscataqua River back to the shipyard.

My father was a boss welder, one of the people in charge. On a personal basis, I suppose he felt guilty. Who knows? He knew a lot of the people who had died—engineers, sailors, and others who were on the sub. I was with him and we watched as they towed the *Squalus* up the river. He never recovered from it. After the *Squalus*, he was never quite the same. He continued working at the yard—my uncle was a machinist there at the time, too—but I think anyone that had anything to do with this ship's building was a changed man after the *Squalus* sunk.

There's a postscript to this story though, one in which our roles reversed: My father eventually retired from the Navy yard and worked for me for thirteen years selling real estate. The day he retired, he came into my office and said, "I just retired. There must be something I can do; sweep the stairs or something." I sent for a license for him, and he got it. That was the beginning of his listening to me. He did everything. When my future wife Marie came to work as an agent in the real estate office, he and my son Joseph took her everywhere and showed her all around the area. That's when the three bonded. He didn't know and I didn't know who Marie was—or would be!—she was just an independent salesperson. He was teaching her the real estate business. My dad got to know Marie before I did, really. My father figuratively put his arm around her and took her in to my real estate business.

I won't deny sometimes my dad would drive me crazy though. Back then, everybody in the office had a CB radio in their car connected to the office. My father would get on the radio and call the office. In those days, everybody in the world could pick up . . . it was a citizen's band, but it was a joke. Everyone could tune in on the "Shanley channel." People could not wait for Joe Shanley's listings because of the CB. Anytime he would have a thought, he'd radio the office. He would be "Joe Shanley" and tell the damnedest things. For example, if he had just listed a house and the husband and wife were fighting, my father would say right over the radio, "I just had an interesting listing and the couple was having a fight. The guy was yelling at his wife to lose weight!" All the secretaries would snicker, and he and I would have an altercation. Naturally, he put up with me, but I never failed to correct him after all those years of him correcting me. Of course, I drove him crazy, but he loved working for me. Underneath it all, he was proud. He worked for me until his end.

Obituary of Joseph J. Shanley

From the *Portsmouth Herald*, July 30, 1974:

Funeral services for Joseph J. Shanley, 72, of 279 Wibird St., were held yesterday from the Farrell Funeral Home.

A Mass of Christian Burial was held at the Church of the Immaculate Conception, celebrated by the Rev. Francis Curran, pastor, and the Rev. Michael Griffin of the Holy Angels Parish, Plaistow, and the rev. Robert P. Phalen, S.J., of Campion Hall, North Andover, Mass.

Seated within the sanctuary were the Rev. Joseph Shields of St. Catherine's Church, the Rev. George Soberick and the Rev. David Scahill of the Church of the Immaculate Conception.

Mrs. Howard Jackson, organist, directed the choir.

John N. Quirk was usher.

Included in the attendance were students and teachers of St. Patrick's Junior High School; N.H. Realtors, headed by William Ball, president; Seacoast Realtors Associations; Portsmouth Lodge of Elks; Retreat Guild; Holy Name Society; Jim Shanley Agency, Inc.; Wentworth Fairways and the Twilight League; Naval Shipyard employes [sic]; Sisters of Lady Isle.

Also Mayor Bruce Graves, former Mayors Andrew H. Jarvis, Eileen D. Foley and Arthur F. Brady, Jr.; Police Commissioners J. Paul Griffin, George Amergian and William Kelley; Judge Thomas E. Flynn; City Clerk Peter E. O'Donnell;

City Treasurer Mrs. Theresa Demarais; City Councilman Richard Chaisson and William F. Keele.

Officers of Portsmouth Trust Company; Portsmouth Housing Authority; Portsmouth Motor Mart; Iafolla Industries; Jarvis Restaurant; G. Warren Wilder of the John Sise Company; Robert Allard representing the Republican City Committee; Ruth Kotsonis, secretary to U.S. Rep. Louis C. Wyman; Judge William F. Harrington; James Sheridan, president of the Parish Council; Regan Electric Company.

Robert Iafolla and Eric Gustafson of the Hospital Board; Frank Bergenthal representing St. Thomas Aquinas High School; National Association of Retired Federal Employes [sic].

The Holy Name Society and the Layman Retreat Guild recited the rosary at the funeral home Tuesday night.

The Portsmouth Lodge of Elks under the direction of Bruce Burkevitch, exalted ruler, conducted services Tuesday evening at the funeral home.

Burial was in the family lot in Calvary Cemetery with Father Scahill conducting the committal and Father Griffin assisting.

Bearers were Joseph, James and Michael Shanley, Jeffrey Hass, John Serino and Frederick McCaffery.

Obituary of Marie G. Shanley

From the *Portsmouth Herald*, September 16, 1986:

Marie G. Shanley, 83, of Wibird St., widow of Joseph J. Shanley, died Sept 16. Funeral from the Farrell Funeral Home, 694 State St. Mass of Christian Burial at the Church of the Immaculate Conception, Wed. at 10:30 a.m. friends invited. No visiting hours. Memorials may be made to the charity of one's choice.

CHAPTER 4

Youth on Wibird Street

I was born January 26, 1928, to Joseph John Shanley and Marie Gertrude McCaffery Shanley. I was the first grandchild for James Andrew McCaffery and Mary Leary McCaffery. I was the first of anyone's children on both sides of the family. My mother called me Jimmy, but most people call me Jim. "He could sell pork chops to a pig," she would always say of me. To neighbors, my mother would say, "Where did I get him from?" I lived all my life with her saying that. She reveled in all my successes, but never said a word. My family was all hard-working, but she couldn't understand my later traveling the world, banking, business. It was alien to her.

Dad and Mom and I lived at 269 Wibird, next door to 279 Wibird. When the time came that 269 was sold, my mother could not leave her mother, and so Dad, she, and I moved in next door to 279 with my grandparents. My sister Mary Ellen came along when I was approximately ten, and Martha when I was fifteen.

My neighborhood set me up for a Norman Rockwell life. Once my grandfather had broken ground, the Irish had flocked in along with everyone else. A Greek family (Marinos) lived across the street; next to them were the Scammons (Yankees). Next were a French family (Dube) and the Maddocks (Yankee).

Behind the Maddocks were the Deitrichs (German). The Griffins (Irish) were across the street, along with the Jarvis family (Greek). The Cummings (Jewish) and the Ashes (Yankees) were there, too; their patriarch was always known as "Tinker Ash." Next were the Managals, another Irish family. Across from them on the corner were the Tuckers (Yankees), the family of a local lawyer. We were a league of nations, and the house was always known in the neighborhood as "279." All the children played in the street. Mothers didn't worry about anyone molesting anyone. There were tough sections of town, but ours was Utopia.

The reader needs to understand that in order to get through the 1929 and early 1930 Great Depression years, our three Irish families lived in one house at 279: my grandparents, my parents and their kids, my mother's brother, Freddy, and his wife, Connie, and later their son, my cousin Freddy. My grandparents took the worst bedroom, at the back second floor. Similar arrangements continued until I went in the Navy in 1945. The house at 279 Wibird Street is still in the McCaffery family.

During the Depression, some other McCaffery relatives moved to Portsmouth from Michigan, all in one car. They slept in the car along the way. They were so dirty when they arrived at 279 that they went upstairs and bathed in the one tub. (I sneaked upstairs and found all the dirt made quite a brown ring on the tub.) One of the men's name was Chili. He became a successful boxer, but I never saw him box. There were eight or more in the car, and I happened to be on the porch when they arrived and piled out. They all eventually found habitation in Portsmouth.

My mother's sister, Margaret, or "Aunt Gargie," lived with us, too, at least until she met her husband. She was a legal secretary and married Leo Power from Roxbury, Massachusetts. They were married at the Women's City Club in Portsmouth and had five children. Like my mother, Gargie couldn't bear to be away from her mother for long. Subsequently, she, Uncle Leo and all the children constantly visited 279 Wibird Street.

Aunt Gargie kept a picture of me in my football uniform on her son's bedroom wall. She would often bring me to Jamaica Plain, where she lived with Uncle Leo. I had never ridden a trolley car before visiting her. When Aunt Gargie rented a house at Wallis Sands on the beach, next door was a judge from Manchester with a family and a gorgeous au pair. I can remember trailing her from behind and finally catching up with her to walk along the beach together.

At the top of the stairs to the left was a little room that was my bedroom. There was a lovely front room occupied by my mother and father. Behind it was another bedroom for Uncle Freddy and his wife, Connie, when she came along. The rear bedroom was occupied by my grandmother and grandfather.

Frederick Gerald, "Freddy," my cousin, whom I love to this day, and I grew up together. He was named after his father and Aunt Connie's brother, also Gerald, an electric company linesman who lost an arm when he was electrocuted (he survived). Cousin Freddy was much younger than I, and Aunt Connie came up every morning and took care of our room. I can remember her bathing him as a baby in the claw-foot tub. Later, he grew to throw a football like a bullet. He went to Portsmouth High School (PHS) and was the quarterback for the PHS football team. His mother and father were taken by me to every football game in Portsmouth in which he played.

When Freddy grew to be maybe ten or twelve years old, my grandfather built two complete rooms in the attic out of sheet-rock—one for each of us. The walls and ceilings were made of a corrugated material held together by approximately three-inch wooden slats. My grandfather sensed the persnickety in me and assigned me the job of varnishing all the slats. I took charge of my own room. It was simply a great opportunity for me to assemble my collections, especially the decals that were given every time a submarine was launched. There were so many of these collections that I proudly placed each of them on the walls of my room. Today the Power children have remained my pals, but they still remember happily destroying my collections.

Hawthorne Street all the way to South Street was owned by an extremely wealthy Yankee family. They owned a mansion on the corner of South and Union streets in Portsmouth. Their land ran from the rear of the mansion at the top of South Street all the way down to Hawthorne Street. They built a building with garages, chauffeur's quarters and helper's quarters. Further down the property, about one hundred yards to the rear of 279, they built a fantastic two-story playhouse for their grandchildren. They surrounded the property with a wooden fence right next to our property. We knew when the children were in there playing. I don't recall if they ever actually played with us outside, but we were never invited inside the playhouse. When the Depression came, they fell on hard times and part of the fence fell down. We finally had a chance to enter the playhouse, as they never locked it! It had two stories and was as big as my house is today. They had everything in this building, even a trapeze! They obviously didn't want their children or grandchildren to go without, but the mansion and garage have now been turned into condominiums.

In the cellar at 279, was an old-fashioned black, pot-bellied stove fed by my father, uncle, and grandfather to heat the three stories above it. There was nothing like my father cooking steaks, lamb chops and pork chops on top of the red coals. The coal was stored under the cellar stairs in the coal bin. When ice cubes were delivered to 279, they were brought to the back door on the deliverer's shoulder pad with a big ice pick. We had a wooden ice box in a little room adjoining the kitchen area.

Friday night dinner was fish from the Blue Fin Fish Market, waffles, and French toast. I have always loved waffles and ate them all the time as a kid with slabs of butter, molasses and New Hampshire maple syrup. It was religion. (I was so amazed recently to see a waffle iron that, if you don't want just two waffles, you flip it over and it makes four!) Aunt Connie would work her tail off and cut single waffles into halves and fourths. We waited all week long for this meal; it was a genuine feast. We'd all be in the same room listening to Father Coughlin on the radio. My grandfather and I would later play cribbage and checkers. My grandmother taught me how to play casino, along with all the tricks of the game, so my fellow sailors never could cheat me.

On Saturday upon coming home from church, my grandmother would have prepared the previous day a crock of baked beans. She would prepare this concoction with buckets of hot dogs and brown bread lathered with butter. There would be some kind of piccalilli sauce. We'd come home to beans, molasses, slabs of pork in the big pot, all the hot dogs you could possibly eat, and fantastic brown bread. The men would drink coffee.

In the years living at 269 and 279, the McCaffery and Shanley men never drank in either home. The exception was a relative Harry Perkins and his wife Olive, who were invited every holiday. My grandmother always made beer available to Harry, but otherwise we never had alcohol in the house. On holidays and Sundays, my grandmother would cook a rare roast beef. When she cut into it, she'd let the blood fill up at the end of the platter and attempt to spoon-feed it to me. Over the years, I hated the experience, but sure enjoyed blood running from charcoal steaks.

At night, we would meet at the kitchen table for dinner. The men were always hungry after spending the day working, and the women would make sure dinner was ready at 4:30 p.m. On Sunday, we always ate in the dining room as a family.

Within the house, there was a strict division of power. My grandmother ruled the kitchen, and my mother and Aunt Connie took care of the rest of the house. There was a massive coal-fired furnace into which my grandfather, father, and uncle would shovel the coal to heat the house—with me eventually joining them as I grew up. I also worked on our lawn and would do some weeding, but not much because it gave my father and grandfather great pride, so they wanted to do it. My dad planted with pride a meticulous garden, especially of vegetables, as each season progressed. Uncle Freddy and Dad planted flowers among large rocks at the back of the vegetable garden. My grandfather planted a series of various bushes along the northern border of his property. He prided himself on 279 and kept it impeccable. He loved his flowers, vegetable garden and various bushes on the side of our house—the same bushes he would chase me around after I would slam the bulkhead to get his attention.

I remember exactly how the cellar was oriented. When you got down the bulkhead steps, to the right were two or three massive wooden bins. My grandmother and grandfather stored bushels of potatoes, squash, and all kinds of vegetables for the winter months. Following these bins was a soapstone double-sink, in which so many things besides washing vegetables occurred. My father eventually installed a half-bath against the back wall. Both he and my grandfather built a massive worktable with various appliances and tools. There was also a storage area, and against the front wall was all of the bottled and canned food. My father and uncle would spend all night long in front of cauldrons boiling bottles, canning the vegetables for the upcoming winter. They would buy bottles by the crate.

The whole backyard was a vegetable garden. My grandfather loved flowers too. When my father first came to Portsmouth, he worked for Governor Spaulding at the Spaulding mansion. He always had an interest in flowers. He built a beautiful rock garden next to the backyard fence.

We had one full bathroom on the second floor of 279— for three families! With my mother's approval, my father added a half-bath in the basement and a second one off the kitchen.

We had a three-quarter wrap-around porch. My grandfather built a screened section to the right and on hot summer nights, I slept out there with my cousin Freddy. There were stairs from the front sidewalk to the porch, and from the front door was a wide hall entering an eating area with adjoining kitchen. To the right was the living room, behind which was the dining room. Next to the kitchen was the panty, which contained all the crockery and dishes and was where my grandmother made her pies. Behind the kitchen was what we called the scullery. It contained a wooden ice box, and every week a man would come in a rickety gas-powered truck with big squares of ice, a leather strap on his shoulders and an ice pick. He would walk up the rear cement stairs, enter the scullery and place the ice. Eventually, I became friends with his family.

My grandmother always got up at 4:00 a.m. and went down to the pantry adjacent to the kitchen to start making mince pies, apricot pies, apple pies and others. My mother, after rising, would be in charge of breakfast, and Aunt Connie would bake and cook her specialties. Beggars would come to the back door and ask for food, which my grandmother always gave them. They'd sit on the back steps and clean their plates. It is told that those poor men had a system of marking the back door or steps of the homes for each other indicating where they could get food on future visits. Uncle Freddy and my father would have left for work to the Portsmouth Naval Yard by 7:00 a.m. and would arrive home very hungry around 4:30 p.m.

The family always had a kitchen table, where I learned many things. In addition to the ice man, a series of people came to the back door. An immigrant peddler from Russia had a big truck filled with goods: potatoes, corn, turnips, seasoning and so on. His nickname was "By Golly" because it was his reply to everything that was said. His children went on to earn fabulous college degrees and became great teachers and musicians. They lived on Cabot Street in Portsmouth, and "By Golly" would come once a week. There was so much produce in his truck it would bounce up and down the street. He would come to the back door and he and my grandmother would exchange money for purchases. They would banter and haggle and have lots of laughs. He really enjoyed the repartee and duking it out with my grandmother over a nickel. Listening to them was an education in business all in itself—they both depended on getting a good deal without taking advantage of the other.

The McCafferys and the Shanleys never charged anything on credit cards; they brought cash and paid up front. Because we were so very, very middle class, I always learned to save. I still have a little desk in my home office from my childhood. It has different slots in it that were used to hold and allocate the money the men brought home. On Friday afternoons when I was a little boy, the men in my family would put their paychecks (mostly cash) on this desk. The three women would then divide it up and put different amounts into the slots that indicated church, groceries, and other obligations. There was always some left for charity; my mother would send ten dollars every month without fail to St. Labre Mission.

My father probably took home forty dollars per week. He had one car, and it was the cheapest Ford you could get. The only entertainment for my parents on Saturday night before there was television was taking the Model T and parking it in front of Newbury's Department Store, where the farmers from Eliot and Kittery ("Elyit" and "Kitry") shopped. They walked and talked differently and dressed in farm clothes. In the meantime, here we were living with no-plaster slats and a potbelly stove in the cellar. We had nothing, but we had a car.

From childhood, I played the card game casino, especially with my Grandmother, and she was sly. As a family, being poor, we played cards a lot. She taught me all about the cheats and how they were maneuvered. One night, our family played it with some neighbors. When one of the ladies palmed a card, I banged down her hand on the table and exposed her. She never came to the house again. My mother and aunt wanted to choke me because it was rude. I was probably seven or eight at the time, but I was a casino player forever!

When I was a little boy in the 1930s, there was an authentic gypsy camp on Sagamore Avenue. Everyone was frightened of gypsies, and people called them "the Roma." Their main occupation was basket-weaving, and they would sell their baskets on the road. The shacks are still there. All parents, including mine, would say, "If you're not good, I'm going to give you to the gypsies." The men all wore earrings and bandanas. They looked fierce to a little boy.

Dr. McGill was the family physician. In those days, when we called the doctor he would arrive in his automobile, enter the house, sit and listen to my mother or aunt as to what the medical

problem was. He was well known for his diagnostic ability. My
grandmother, mother, or aunt would tell him about Little Jimmy.
When I saw his car drive up, I would run out the back door and
climb the massive pine tree in the rear yard. I would sit on a limb
hoping he would leave. He would often outwait me or wait until
my father and Uncle Freddy came home from the Navy Yard.
My father would say "Jimmy, come down," and I did what I was
told. (My family to this day has always called me "Jimmy," and
the grandchildren "Grampa Jim.") They would gently put me in
the car, follow Dr. McGill's car down to his second floor office
on Congress Street. He would sharpen a needle and give me an
injection for whatever inoculation was necessary. He was loved a
lot by other doctors and the public.

My father's siblings visited often. Uncle Paul Shanley to the
best of my knowledge never married but had numerous girlfriends
and lived in the Shanley family home in Brighton, Massachusetts.
Uncle Paul was an accountant with the city of Boston. He immediately took a shine to my first wife, Joanne, and subsequently
to my second wife, Marie. He was a supreme bridge player and
played it avidly. He had lots of thoughts about what he was going
to do with his nephew and like to express them. When Uncle
Paul became older with the attendant illnesses of old age, my
sister Mary Ellen really befriended him. She took him to doctors'
appointments and visited him in the hospital, as we all did. He
had many friends and would often take trips with them and his
girlfriends.

My father's sister, Aunt Mary, was a shop girl. She met Bob
McConnell, who was the manager of the Lincoln Department
Store, a small store in Newburyport, Massachusetts. They fell in
love, married and had two sons. Bob was a taciturn, quiet man,
and they would summer at the cottages on Rye Beach facing the

ocean. When I lived in the attic at 279, Aunt Mary and Uncle Bob bought me my first radio, which I prized.

Schooling

I went to Lafayette School for kindergarten before entering St. Patrick's Catholic school for first through ninth grade. I started school in knickers, those awful things!

I was nine years an altar boy at Immaculate Conception Church. My mother and Aunt Connie would sometimes drive me to the church with my washed, ironed cassock. Other times I would walk with the cassock from Wibird Street to the church. We got up very early, and I know I got fed because they sure took great care of me. We had a brief breakfast together, and then my father and uncle were picked up out front quite promptly at 7 a.m. by two other men for work. My mother and Aunt Connie would get in their crappy black car and go to Mass. They went through snow, rain—anything. There was a group of elderly Catholic men and a lot of women who went every day. They were all over fifty and would go to church with the one priest celebrating Mass.

On a typical day, I was an altar boy at the 7:15 a.m. Mass. My mother wanted me to be a priest, no question about it. She would press my cassock; anytime there was a spot on it, my mother would insist I bring it home for her to wash.

On high holidays, my blouse would be all lace, and we would hold burning candles attached to the top of the brass candlesticks. We would be honor guards on the altar and generally the priest who had celebrated Mass would march behind us.

I learned about funerals at a young age. In the Catholic School, the nuns would make us feel good if someone in our family died. They told us, "Don't worry, our Lord will raise friends, parents, grandparents, and all good people, and at the end we all will meet on the Plains of Abraham." I would say, "Sister? How are we all going to fit?"

In later years when I became stronger, I was appointed among the other altar boys to stand guard at a funeral. The casket was brought down the aisle toward the rear followed by weeping women and teary-eyed men. The pallbearers were first and the casket passed us, followed by the priest sprinkling holy water and finally, the mourners. We would stand in formation while the casket was being put in the funeral hearse and then head to school.

As an altar boy, the only good thing about funerals was that I didn't have to go to school until the funeral was over. Even though I didn't have to go to school for those two hours, experiencing all those funerals has haunted me all my life.

After a few years, I became an altar boy server. The priest would perform Mass on the altar in Latin, and the other boy and I would get the holy water and wine. In the middle of Mass, people would come to the altar for a wafer representing the body of Jesus Christ, and I got to hold the chalice for the priest.

Everyone in those days went to confession on Saturday afternoons at three o'clock. The confessional was a box at the back of the church where the priest would listen to people's sins and give them penance. The other little boys and I enjoyed going to confession on Saturday afternoons at the Immaculate Conception Church because we knew we would see Mary Jane Hazzard—my future wife's sister and a ravishing beauty. We boys would gawk at her walking up the aisle to the confessional and then approaching all of us as she proceeded down the aisle to kneel at the alter and pray for the sins she had just confessed. We had never seen anything like her and would stare at the vision of this beautiful girl. We knew she would come every Saturday to confess her sins.

Like most Catholics, I believe we had the same sins every week.

After Mass, I would go St. Patrick's School next door, where I went steadily for nine years. Upon reflection, the nuns gave us one hell of an education, as shown by the class leaders we had in public high school. I loved the nuns, and why wouldn't they love the boy with the brick-red hair? They fostered the competition between me and Dickie Delamura.

Religious education was good for me. I listened to the nuns. I spent nine years in Catholic School, and there's no question the nuns, my father, mother, grandmother, and grandfather built in me forever integrity and to always tell the truth. It was constantly apparent; I never knew anything else. Some of the guys at school would be naughty in the nun's opinion and get the retan (a leather strap) on the palm of their hand. The nun would (gently) whack them, and they'd go back to their seat. I never got it. I was never a saint by any stretch of the imagination, but my parents never had to go and talk to the nuns about my behavior.

Every Friday afternoon in eighth grade, if I didn't measure up to Sister DeLord's standards, she would tell me to "Go Home"—she'd had enough of me for the week. I would march up Marston Avenue until I met up with my friend's mother, Mrs. Cabrera, who knew I'd been sent out by the sister. Mrs. Cabrera kept this secret with me; she knew behind the scenes that I had been reprimanded. I'd stand out in the yard with her and she'd tell me stories until I could go home without being too early. She told me she'd married a Spanish guy who rode with an army in South America. Years later, Joanne and I once visited Sister DeLord with our children when she retired to the Sisters of Mercy Home in Windham, New Hampshire. Obviously, she just loved Jimmy Shanley and his gang of children.

St. Patrick's was predominantly an Irish-Catholic elementary school. We had a few French and Polish students, but it was mostly Irish kids who went there. Dunkin O'Brien (known as "Dunky") was a strong, wiry guy who would take me on in the courtyard, which was really nothing but the street. One time, we were having a fight and he picked me up and drove me into the ground. On it was a board with a big spike, which went straight into my head. The Sister and my classmates carried me into the nunnery before rushing me to the Portsmouth Hospital. I can vividly remember the doctor putting his knees on my shoulders and pulling the nail out. He applied antiseptic and bandaged me up. Maybe it was just a nail, but my memory from childhood is that it was a spike. But I survived, and Dunky and I have had laughs as the years passed.

I took pride in doing my homework, and oftentimes my father would review it. I wouldn't call them heated debates, but he expected perfection. He was an eighth-grade graduate. He was a smart guy though, and valued education for me.

Outside school, we all played sports. I formed a baseball team of pals, and we played at Lafayette School baseball field. We formed a league of sandlot baseball teams all over Portsmouth at places like the Whipple School and the Haven School. We had individual team names and constantly competed. I kept track of it all for my team, and the *Portsmouth Herald* let me write up reports on this "league." I was organized as a little boy. This was from say seven, eight and nine years old. We were just kids being kids. My mother and my wife Joanie always marveled how I kept track of runs, hits, and so on. I found my book in the cellar in the corner; I still have it, and a couple of friends who played with me are still alive.

The biggest physical pain I ever experienced was when I broke my arm skating on North Mill Pond. Dr. McGill set it. It was excruciating. We played hockey on the pond. If you walked up the hill from Wibird Street there was "first pond" and "second pond" in the woods. Second pond was famous for me because I loved pick-up hockey. Our hockey games were mano-a-mano. When frozen, the ponds were always open. I don't know what has changed, although the climate is probably not as cold.

Emerson Reid was an African American, and he would play hockey with us. He was the first African American I knew as a young boy. I was a ferocious hockey player as a young man, but always remembered how I sat on the bank of the pond, with him kneeling down and tying up my skates. I idolized him. He later became a track star. Emerson's kindness has always stayed with me. He would have been in his nineties now. The Reids are still in town.

I always wanted to own a .22 rifle. My mother and father were opposed. One day Aunt Connie put me in the car and took me to a place in Kittery that sold guns and ammunition. I had some money saved and put the cash in my pocket. The rifle I always wanted to own was this fantastic one that fed bullets from a tube underneath; it was a magnificent weapon. Naturally, my father and mother were aghast, but they let me keep it.

In those days, people carried guns openly. I would roam around the Lady Isle School area across from the Portsmouth Naval Shipyard and bang away at crows. I never hit one; I never shot an animal. I would pretend to be a hunter and march around with my rifle. I would also ride my bike or walk to Kittery, where there was a pond full of beautiful daylilies that I could pick for my mother. I'd march all over Portsmouth with buckets of .22 shells without any training at all. Mostly, boys had shotguns looking for turkeys. There was a lot of hunting.

There were also tall pine trees in our yard. Oftentimes, Uncle

Freddy (who had been in the Army) and I would go up to my bedroom in the attic, open the window facing a set of the massive pines, and bang away, shooting pine cones off the trees. We were right in the middle of town, and Belle Isle was filled with nuns who could have been hit by our bullets. I don't know what we were thinking—we could have killed someone.

When I was in the Navy, Frederick and Paul Power (one of my wonderful hellion cousins) were fooling around in the attic when Paul accidentally shot Frederick in the leg with my rifle. When I got home from the Navy, my father wouldn't tell me what he had done with the gun. I never saw it again.

Boy Scout

My Boy Scout Scoutmaster for Troop 158 was Robert Murphy of 980 South Street. I was patrol leader and scribe in 1941. I earned the following merit badges: cycling, physical development, cooking, reptile study, woodwork, reading, handicraft and scholarship. I rose to be a Star Scout. I got my uniform at Lothrops, Farnham & Co. in Dover, N.H. Our meetings were held in the basement of St. Patrick's School. We were sponsored by the Immaculate Conception Church. I had a great relationship with the other scouts, and we went to various Boy Scout camps.

He was a great Scoutmaster. Once, a friend of his loaned him the use of a cottage and the surrounding grounds. It was a cottage on Great Bay in Newington, and he had a rowboat tied to his dock. We were allowed free rein. Since I knew how to row, two other scouts and I got in the rowboat one day and off we rowed—with no knowledge of the infamous currents of the Piscataqua River flowing from Great Bay to the Atlantic Ocean. We got caught in a current, and it was so strong there was no way to row out of the current. I'm not saying I wasn't frightened, but the other two scouts started screaming like little girls. A small motor launch came up the river with enough power to seize the prow and lasso us. He lassoed it to his boat and pulled us up to the dock. It was a big blotch on the Scoutmaster; he hadn't given us permission, we just got in the boat and left. All the scouts and the Scoutmaster were on the dock when we returned, and by God, they were cheering! They had called the Sheriff's Department, so waiting for us were two Rockingham County sheriffs. We were all obviously relieved not to have drowned.

My mother and father, though living in tough times, sent me to Camp Carpenter. A camp counselor was going to teach me to swim so I could finally become an Eagle Scout. As instructed, I jumped off the dock, dove down, and came up under an adjacent wooden raft. It was the fright of a lifetime, and I never did learn to swim, even after joining the Navy. I sure can paddle, though.

One of the camping trips with the Scoutmaster was for an extended long weekend in Wolfeboro, N.H. We were probably eighteen in number. We had the normal activities during the first day, and the Scoutmaster had made arrangements with a doctor and a friend to shepherd us for one night. The doctor and his friend arrived in a station wagon and parked adjacent to the campsite; they were forced to sleep in it while the scouts stayed in tents. As boys do, we raised holy hell all night. We finally went to bed and let them have their "rest." In subsequent years, the doctor and his pal would regale me with tales of their sleepless night camping with the troop—apparently they each took turns being "on patrol" all evening.

On Memorial Day, I would be assigned to hang onto the leather strap that held the American Flag in front of our scout troop. We would assemble at Parrot and Junkins avenues and march up Market Street to Market Square. From there we would go down Islington Street to Richards Avenue, with me hanging onto the flag. We marched to the North Cemetery and listened to speeches about the history of Portsmouth. Taps were played before we marched back.

Boy Scouts connects generations. My sons still talk about the Pinewood Derby races, where sons and fathers build wooden race cars together. I purchased lead weights to make them roll faster. I took my sons' Pinewood Derby cars to the drugstore to make sure they weighed within the allowed weight range. I was trying to teach my boys the lesson: always be honest. There were boys' cars disqualified for being overweight because their fathers cheated and their cars were too heavy. I taught my boys to obey the rules.

The Dowager

When I was about nine, my neighbor next door said to me one day, "I'd like to have you weed my garden. I'll pay you ten cents an hour." It was a bitch. I soon said to my grandfather, "May I borrow your lawnmower?" It was a push mower, not powered, except by me. Within approximately a year, I had accumulated thirteen neighbors as clients. I cut their lawns and trimmed their bushes, etc., on a regular weekly basis. I scheduled all of it myself. My grandfather would take the mower to a machine shop in Portsmouth to have the blades sharpened. The cost was on my grandfather—nice man that he was!

I kept that business going through high school and saved all the money I made. I would walk to and from my jobs, take the bus to Rye, or a neighbor would sometimes pick me up and drive me. I always knew I could turn to my family if I needed help; my Dad and Uncle would often help me after work at the Navy Yard. My mother would take me to deposit the earned money in the Piscataqua Savings Bank, where they had a big stuffed bear in the lobby.

Before I was born, my mother became the office manager/receptionist for Dr. Blaisdel, a dentist who owned the mansion on the top of Wibird Street that is now Edgewood, a big nursing home. My mother introduced me to Dr. Blaisdel and his wife, and I started mowing for them. They were kind enough to let me use their equipment. What intrigued me was their superb goldfish pond, which started my lifelong fascination with fish tanks. I loved going there.

During all my formative years, a husband and wife in Rye had a small estate, and they also hired me to keep the grounds. I would take the bus from Portsmouth to Rye when I was in middle school and take care of the property. It was impossible for me, usually arriving at 8 a.m. and working all day long, to finish the job. Because of my age, my father and uncle would come down in the family flivver and help me finish, not because I asked but because they loved me. The job was accomplished in one day with their help, and that went on weekly.

One of my customers was Mrs. Borthwick. She was the widow of Mr. Borthwick, who owned Borthwick's Department Store—the biggest competitor of French's Department Store next door. My mother would take me to both stores occasionally, when we saved enough money to buy sheets, etc.

We lived in a community ruled by Yankees. Mrs. Borthwick lived on the corner of Hawthorne and Wibird and dressed like a Yankee widow, all in black and white with a little hat. She sat at the corner window of her house where she could survey her entire lot and the three lots surrounding her home. She would watch me work and every afternoon pay me in cash from her little Yankee purse with a clasp at the top.

I took care of her property for a long time. When I went into business in the '50s, it hadn't been that many years since there were deeds that read "No Irish or Jews." Mrs. Borthwick owned the "Orchard," which ran all the way from Middle Road to the by-pass. The Portsmouth Redevelopment Corporation (PRC) wanted to buy the land and found they weren't getting anywhere with her. I was an Irish Catholic, and my friend and client Harry Weinbaum was the rising Jewish star. Harry came to Portsmouth on a train. He was a boxer and founded Weinbaum News Service. He was a successful businessman. When he got interested in real estate, he knew that if he dealt with me (as he often did), I'd represent him fairly. I went to high school with his son, Sumner, and we were on the Portsmouth High School football team together, so we had some history. However, as far as PRC was concerned, I was the token Irishman and Harry was the token Jew—they may not have known then that I represented Harry in various real estate transactions.

I've had many wonderful mentors, but Bradford Kingman was one in particular. He was born in Durham, New Hampshire, and was President of the Portsmouth Trust Company. He came to my office one day, sat on my red couch and asked "Jim, would you consider becoming a director on the Portsmouth Redevelopment Corporation?" He also mentioned that he was going to approach Harry Weinbaum about joining. I said "Sure would." A subsequent meeting was set up to talk with Mrs. Borthwick again about selling her property to the PRC.

Meeting in Mrs. Borthwick's living room to see about buying her property, all the Yankees sat up front while Harry and I were put in the back. She looked over their heads and said, "Is that Jimmy Shanley back there? Jimmy, come up and sit with me." She then told everyone she was going to turn all her real estate over to me to manage the development. Who would have guessed that little Jimmy would bring the Portsmouth Hospital, Liberty Mutual and so many others to the Orchard area? It all started with my grandfather's push mower, but Mrs. Borthwick was the fuse that finally lit my rocket.

Sometime later, Bradford and the Board of Directors invited Harry and me to join the Portsmouth Trust Company as Directors. We proudly accepted.

Always working

In high school, I had a lot of jobs. I was working at the Portsmouth Naval Shipyard as a laborer during World War II on the construction of the submarines. At the end of World War II, my father had eight hundred welders working for him at the Shipyard. They sure built many subs during the War. The Navy reports of the Portsmouth Naval Shipyard submarines' exploits make fascinating reading.

We were desperate—women were working there for the first time; Rosie the Riveter and all of that. I was a little squirt, so when one of the men purposely dropped a tool, they'd send me down into the bowels of the sub to get it, then and close the hatch with me inside. There I was; the son of Joe Shanley, the boss; and they're going to teach me, me and my mouth . . . they knew my father would be making the rounds so they posted spotters. And they knew I would never squeal on them. It was sure scary. I guess it dawned on them after a couple of times that it wasn't fun anymore.

After work one day, a pal from Berlin, New Hampshire, and I walked along Miller Avenue and then sat on the granite curbing in front of Dr. Griffin's house. He was a retired dentist. All of a sudden, a police car with lights flashing swerved in and pinned my pal and me. The cops got out, grabbed us, and dragged us into Dr. Griffin's bedroom. He was elderly, in poor health and in bed, and pointed at the two of us. "Those are the burglars!" he accused. What had happened previously was, in some manner, Dr. Griffin was robbed. We were taken to the local police station and brought before the sergeant in charge. He took one look at us and said, "What is Jimmy McCaffery's grandson doing here"? The officers told of Dr. Griffin's accusation, and the sergeant said, "Just take Jimmy home." They put my pal on a bus back to Berlin.

Unfortunately, I found girls, and sports. While I was fairly bright, I was interested more in girls and sports than my studies. I was a superb football player and second baseman. In basketball, since I was short, Coach Ralph Lizzio would put me in when he needed someone to slug it out. We also played many sports on the street in front of 279.

The May house on Middle Street was a historical estate with a massive yard facing its rear to St. Patrick's School. My father before me tried to convince Mr. May, a Boston stockbroker, to sell part of the land so St. Patrick's could have a playground. In subsequent years, I approached him with this idea, too. He was one of those scions of Yankeeville but a very pleasant man. I carried on for my dad and failed; the playing field has never been built and the children still play on the street in front of St. Patrick's School.

In addition to my yard work and work at the Navy Yard, I also worked for the post office while in high school. Mr. Hickey was the Postmaster and World War II was raging. I would get my empty mailbag back to the post office after running around like a crazy man to get the mail delivered. Ninety-nine percent of houses had a mail slot; very few people had mail boxes. I participated in all three sports—football, basketball, and baseball—and delivered the mail after practice. People complained about their mail arriving sometimes at night, but fortunately for me, Postmaster Hickey ignored them.

About the same time, I learned auctioneering from Mr. Cook, who would sell anything. My initial job was simple: show the items to the bidders and collect the money. As he grew older, he delegated the auctioneering to me as well.

The Game

A lifetime accomplishment was made when I was seventeen—in the first post-World War II football championship, between archrivals Portsmouth and Dover. Six thousand people came to Cowell Stadium at UNH to see this game, and I scored the two winning touchdowns. A horrible war had been raging, so any entertainment was good. Historically, Dover and Portsmouth had an intense rivalry in every sport. "Dover by the smell; Portsmouth by the sea" was our popular saying. (The "smell" was on account of the mills in Dover, most long since closed.) I believe as young men, if we bumped into a Dover male, we'd ask if he'd recently had a bath, or just block our noses!

Though one of the smallest players, I was also one of the fastest. I never hit it off on a personal basis with the football coach. I played on the team from 1943 to 1945 as left running back. Since a football field is made up of intervals of ten yards, the coach would graduate members of the squad from one ten-line to another. He would have me run the gauntlet and the guys were to tackle me. I was always either #1 or #2 boy in terms of grades right through the ninth grade, fighting it out for the top spot with my pal Dickie Delamura (who later became an admiral and pilot.)

On the high school team, there was one player who never really liked me, and he couldn't wait for practice so he could tackle and pound me. Most of the time I would get through the line, but this guy and another fellow were bigger than me, and I was a skinny little kid. I didn't dread it; it was all part of the challenge, even if I knew I was dead meat. The purpose was to teach, and our job was to learn to avoid the opponent. We'd carry home our dirty football shirts and our mothers would wash them. I can clearly remember walking up Richards Avenue with my dirty uniform. We would leave the practice field on Parrot Avenue and go from Richards to Islington to Wibird Street.

The coach put up with me because I was greased lightning and obviously loved playing football. I also played as safety on defense, or, when I was running on the offense, as left half-back. Dover's star running back was a boy named Ernie; he was built like a steamroller. I remember vividly that nothing pleased our coach. He wanted to win, and he wanted Ernie stopped. Ernie was a brick tank, and he would come through his line and run in the open field. I was the safety and the last person every time he came through. He had to get by me to reach the goal line, and I was damned if he was going to score a touchdown. It was like a steamroller hitting a wall. There would be an explosion, and we would end up on the ground every time, as I remember it. I can still picture Ernie coming through the line . . . I hit him and he went on his ass! That memory and the memory of my crashing over the goal for the two touchdowns to beat Dover 12-6 replay in my mind to this day. My father had never seen me perform, but that Thanksgiving Day he got my grandfather to join him. Underneath it all, they were always admiring, but I remember that day how proud they were standing there. With all the tribe around, it was an unforgettable Thanksgiving dinner.

For some reason, we weren't recognized as state champions at the time—maybe something to do with the confusion of the war—and the team as well as the community were NOT happy. Here was a memorable game—the epitome of local football at that time. Forever, the rivalry was there. The stands were full. It was a humiliating defeat for Dover because we weren't big guys. Though we didn't get a banner, the *Portsmouth Herald* sports page had great writing and sure satisfied our egos.

When the game was finished and Thanksgiving dinner was over with the tribe, Joanie-(already my girlfriend) and I rushed to get a copy of the *Herald*. Newspaper reporters say the write-up of that game by Bob Kennedy was classic as to what reporters wrote at that time. It's amazing to me how the author of the article— forever on my den wall!—describes Portsmouth versus Dover right after the end of World War II. I think he called me "Little Red." The article symbolizes a method of writing that doesn't exist in 2014. It was a heartfelt story of what they saw in the stands as we went on to victory for Portsmouth High School.

Decades later, I was driving in the mountains of California when my car phone rang. Eddie Anania was the right halfback on the PHS football team while I was the left halfback. His nephew was calling me, upset that his father's team was not recognized at the school for winning the 1945 state championship. He wanted to do something about it and organized a team. I gave him a copy of the article reporting the game when I returned home. He made a presentation for the high school to receive its winning banner, which is now in the high school auditorium.

The dedication ceremony was a remembrance celebration of the victory on November 23, 1945. They lugged me out with my son James hanging on to me. He brought me to the fifty-yard line, where they recognized me as a representative of the team.

Those who were still alive assembled at a Portsmouth game. The newspaper covered it again, this time more as a feature than a sports article.

With the war still raging up until the summer of 1945, I had wanted to drop out of high school and join the military earlier, but my father wouldn't let me enlist when I was seventeen. Thank God my father made me finish high school. I turned eighteen soon after that memorable game and reported to the draft board for my physical, enlisting in the U.S. Navy the day after I graduated.

Honoring the Champs

From the *Portsmouth Herald*, December 5, 2010:

PHS seeks to honor '45 football champs

By Mike Sullivan

When you walk into Portsmouth High School's Stone Gymnasium, the rich athletic tradition is obvious. Banners blanket the walls of the gym, paying tribute to great teams of Clippers past. Lifelong city resident Peter Anania, PHS Class of 1973, has always enjoyed looking up at the banners, a few of which he helped bring there as a captain of the track team in the early 1970s.

There was always something missing, though. See, Peter's uncle, Ed Anania, now 82½ years young and a Maryland resident for more than 60 years, was a member of the PHS football team in the 1940s. Peter remembered "Uncle Eddie" talking about one team in particular, the squad that won the 1945 Class B state championship in rather memorable fashion.

It was a Thanksgiving Day contest against Dover, and the teams played old-fashioned, smash-mouth football at Lewis Field on the University of New Hampshire campus in Durham.

"It rained a ton," Eddie Anania recalled last week from his home in Maryland. "You can't imagine using that football field. It seemed like a foot of rain. It was messy."

The mess didn't deter fans from coming out, though, as approximately 6,000 people turned out for the game. An impressive number, and hard to conceive in this day and age when inclement weather shuts towns down and sends people into their storm cellars with handheld devices and cases of bottled water.

"Can you imagine?" Peter Anania asked. "Six thousand people in the pouring rain? That's a big deal."

And while Peter Anania knew quite well the story of this particular big deal, one that saw Portsmouth earn a 14-6 victory to become kings of Class B, there was no acknowledgement of it on the gym walls. It was as though that 1945 championship never existed. That didn't sit well with Peter Anania. "These guys won a champion-ship and nobody knew about it," he said. "That's a shame."

The 1911 football team is up there on the walls, but then nothing until 1964. Many folks probably just figured PHS football fell on hard times, or maybe there wasn't a program. In 1945

World War II was at its tail end but the Cold
War was going on overseas, and the Korean
War wasn't far off. People's minds were probably
occupied with things other than championship
banners. Even Eddie Anania, as well as many of
his PHS teammates, went straight into the service
after graduation. Suffice to say, none of them
were around for a banner-raising ceremony the
following school year, when such occasions tradi-
tionally take place.

Time passed. Years turned to decades. Still,
Peter Anania never let go of that empty feeling of
knowing his uncle's team wasn't properly recognized. "About a year ago I stopped by my uncle's
house and asked why nothing had ever been
done," Peter Anania said. "He really didn't know
why. But I told him I was going to try."

When Anania brought the plight of the 1945
championship team to PHS Athletic Director
Rus Wilson, it was a no-brainer from Wilson's
standpoint. "We couldn't go back and check any
records because the NHIAA only has information
dating back to 1957," Wilson said. "But we're
happy to hear about it. If somebody wants to do
the work and find other champions, we're happy
to add more numbers."

Wilson's only requirement, obviously, is
proving it. "As long as they have reasonable proof
that it happened, we're thrilled to recognize these
older teams."

Find proof Peter Anania did. He contacted

Jim Shanley Sr., who it's fun to note was not yet
"Sr." when the 1945 championship game took
place, and it turned out Shanley still had the old
Portsmouth Herald article on the game. That's a
long time to hold onto a newspaper clipping, but
the fact Shanley scored both Portsmouth touchdowns in the game may have something to do
with it. That article right there is a keeper.

The article was written by Bob Kennedy and
published in the Friday evening, Nov. 23, 1945,
edition and the headline appropriately stated,
"PHS Drowns Dover 14-6."

The lead is priceless, as it reflects a writing
style from generations past.

"Firing all tubes, fore and aft, like the world
famous Portsmouth-built submarines, Portsmouth
High's fighting Clippers dove deeply beneath the
surface of the water on Lewis Field, Durham,
yesterday morning to torpedo the powerful Green
Wave of Dover and sink (Dover Coach Ollie)
Adams' charges 14-6 beneath the rippling waves,
which fans believe constitutes the gridiron at the
University of New Hampshire."

Eddie Anania remembers the game quite
well, as well as head coach Jim Culberson, who
Anania called "a real taskmaster." He also remembers his teammates, and specifically, their size.

"We were a very light team," Eddie said
with a chuckle. "I was 145 pounds and I was the
starting halfback. We were all light, including the
line."

They found a way to win, though, rain and mud be darned. Now, 65 years later, the Clippers have been told they will take their rightful place among other PHS champions on the wall at Stone Gymnasium. Wilson said it would be added likely in time for a fall 2011 pep rally, which members of the 1945 team would be welcomed at.

It's safe to say the 1945 Class B champion Portsmouth High football team will never again be forgotten. Uncle Eddie's nephew made sure of it.

PHS Drowns Dover 14–6 In Mire of Durham

From the *Portsmouth Herald*, November 29, 1945:

PHS Drowns Dover 14–6 In Mire of Durham
By Bob Kennedy

Firing all tubes fore and aft, like the world famous Portsmouth-built submarines, Portsmouth High's fighting Clippers dove deeply beneath the surface of the water on Lewis Field, Durham, yesterday morning to torpedo the powerful Green Wave of Dover and sink Adams' charges 14-6 beneath the rippling waves, which fans believe constitutes the gridiron at the University of New Hampshire.

It may have rained all day, but Ollie Adams and his charges thought that Coach Jim Culberson and his greatest PHS football team snowed them under with a barrage of line smashes and end runs.

Through an unfortunate fumble, Portsmouth allowed the Green Wave to move into the offensive early. It was only a matter of minutes, however, before the boys in red (later the boys in mud) took complete charge of the contest and ran the Green Wave ragged for the second Thanksgiving in succession.

Shanley, O'Leary Shine

Portsmouth's power offensive, sparked by Jim Shanley who tallied two Portsmouth touchdowns and Jack O'Leary, another junior, rolled up better than 200 yards from scrimmage to outrush Dover nearly 4-1, something no other team has been able to do this season. In statistics as well as scoring Portsmouth completely ducked Dover high team in the sopping puddles on the . . .

All-Star PHS Team Aids Jim Shanley In Scoring 2 Touchdowns—O'Leary Stands Out—Locals Outrush Dover 4-1

(continued from Page One) rain-swept field before 6,000 fans, who were just as wet as the players on the gridiron.

The breaking waves were dashing high against the goal posts at the west end of the field when the Clippers took over on their own 18 as the second quarter started. Their offensive had been sputtering and fuming due to dampness in the Clipper motor. However, Dover was leading 6-0 and the kinks just had to be removed.

Jack O'Leary opened the Portsmouth offensive as he raised his periscope and fired one. Number one was good for a 20-yard smash over Meserve of Dover and a first down on the Dover 38, Jack then fired two and it was good for a four-yard gain. It was that flying redhead's turn next. Jim Shanley fired three by snaking through the Portsmouth right tackle, Dick Dalla Mura, for eight yards and a first down on the midfield stripe.

Portsmouth's attack was rolling now and Dover called for time out. After the rest, Charlie Smith picked up a yard and Jack O'Leary let loose with another salvo by punching through the Dover right guard for eight. Jim Shanley came in for his turn again and scurried around the Portsmouth right end as though he were in a hurry for that turkey dinner, and made a first down on the Dover 34. The backs were getting some wonderful holes to dive through from their springboards in back of the line, thanks the cooperation of that marvelous Clipper forward wall, which literally rammed Dover noses into the mud. And, the Dover players looked it when they came up for air. The Portsmouth kids came in for their share of dunkings, too.

With second down and one to go on the Dover 25, powerful Jack O'Leary rammed through the center of the Dover line for 10 yards and a first down on the 15. Charlie Smith, taking a short snap from center from Bob Lovett, lost the wet ball for a moment but recovered a fumble on the 15. On the next play the pigskin was handed to Shanley and the "ole" redhead slammed his way over the Dover goal in a 15-yard spring which just about dried the sod underneath his feet. He got some nice interference from Dick Dalla Mura and Paul Harvey on this run too.

Zany Day, Zany Play
Then came the play which won the game. It was a zany day and this was a zany play. The score was tied at 6-all and this play was an important one. Eddie Anania and Jack O'Leary went back to the 12-yard line as the latter was to try for a placement. The pass from Lovett went to Eddie but the little fellow saw the ball squirt from his hands like orange juice from a squeezer. He ran

over, scooped up the ball and enough water to fill a pail and started for the goal. He was hit by three Dover players on the 5-yard line and then flipped a lateral to Jack O'Leary who was racing along behind. Jack scampered across the goal and Portsmouth was ahead 7-6.

Dover was in a fighting mood but the Portsmouth submarines kept torpedoing all attacks and the half ended with the Clippers still in the lead.

As the drenched boys returned to the field for the second half one could almost sense that the Clippers were determined to keep "those Dover guys away from our territory." And, how they did!

Those Dover boys just couldn't move from their own 33 after Don Smith had raised the kickoff down to the 30. After trying to unplug the Portsmouth dike for three plays, Dick Bolduc went back to punt. He was a little slow getting the ball off and Dick Dalla Mura partially blocked the boot. The pigskin didn't bounce long. For it floated in a puddle "somewhere in the Dover territory" near the 39. Three Portsmouth players went after the ball but it was like bobbing for apples, and Ed Gitschier finally recovered for Dover.-However, it was not a first down and Portsmouth took over.

That O'Leary-Shanley corporation again began to raise heck with Dover shipping. After Jack had dropped a yard Shanley pierced the Dover line for 11 yards, just inches short of a first down. Jack then made it a first on the Dover 27. Jack whammed his way on the next play by speeding between Lovett and Turci for 19 yards and a first down on the Dover 8. Shanley crossed the Dover 4 as he smacked face down in a tremendous puddle.

The Clippers were momentarily halted when O'Leary fumbled on the Dover 4 and Jannelle recovered. Ed Gitschier punted out to the 22 and Portsmouth began to roll again. In three plays O'Leary banged to the 12 but Charlie Smith dropped eight yards as the Dover line swam through to dunk him on the 18. Jim Shanley made up all the yardage lost, however, as he bucked off tackle to the Dover 2 and then carried across the goal on the next play for his, and Portsmouth's, second touchdown. Jack O'Leary using an orthodox running play this time, smashed over Ronnie Pecunies for the point after and the game clincher, 14-6/.

Dover Scores Early

As usual, Dover struck early in the contest and threw a scare into all Portsmouth folks at the game, with the exception of that fighting bunch of rain-soaked kids on the field. Gutrschier had punted to Ed Anania on the ninth play of the game and the petite Clipper was down on his own 15. Jack O'Leary started off right tackle and the ball squirted from his hands on the 20 to be recovered by Capt. Jim Tsimikles of Dover.

Dick Bolduc pounded out two yards and

Clayton Skelly took the ball from Billy Keays on a fake reverse to scoot through the Portsmouth line 18 yards for the six-pointer. It was the same play which had won the game for the Green Wave against Rochester on the same type of day. Bob Meserve's trust-iron shod toe went into the dog house for the morning as his kick went into Umpire Dan Fowler's arms underneath the crossbar, for no go.

There was only one other time in the contrast when the Adamsmen threatened the Clippers. Late in the second quarter Portsmouth took over a punt on its own 18. The Clippers were penalized five yards for offside and on the next play were given a 15-yard penalty to their own 1-yards marker for offensive holding.

O'Leary pulled Portsmouth out of the hole by a nice punt which went dead on the Portsmouth 35. Two plays later Charlie Smith, that brilliant Portsmouth quarterback who led his club to victory yesterday, intercepted a Skelly pass on his own 44. Jack O'Leary got away for a 27-yard gallop to the Dover 30 just as the half ended. And, by the way, this was the longest run of the day.

Fourth period play was dominated by Portsmouth as the hard-rushing Clipper line shoved the Dover backs beneath the surface of the playing field.

By swamping Dover yesterday on the Durham marshes, the Clippers clinched the Class

B championship of New Hampshire despite the fact that Stevens High of Claremont boasts an undefeated team.

Eh! What was that? Did you ask if it rained yesterday?

Clippers Are Masters On Wet or Dry Gridiron
Portsmouth High's Clippers, "masters of speed and deception on a dry field" won a 14-6 gridiron victory yesterday morning over Dover," favored to win on straight power if the field is wet," on a University of New Hampshire field that was much better suited for water polo.

It was an amphibious operation all the way with the famed Green Wave shattering itself on the shoal of a courageous Clipper line.

Shortly before game time Carl Lundholm, director of athletics at the University of New Hampshire, was heard to remark that "that field's a meadow."

By the start of the second half it was more than that, it was a sea of mud and water.

Despite the downpour, and the weather during most of the game was just that, about 6,000 football pecans (charitable term for nuts) filled the stands to capacity and got drenched for their pains.

The lure of a roofed and comparatively dry press box proved too much for many of them. There were perhaps half a dozen working press men there yet the population of the press box as the game started was about 65. At half time that grew to nearer 100. Beside it, a sardine can would have looked like the plains of Kansas.

The water became so deep in parts of the playing field during the second half that you could follow the ball carrier by the wake he left behind him and it was agreed that it was only fitting that the field judge should be Dan Fowler of Exeter, Philips Exeter academy swimming coach and life-saving instructor.

It was a wonder he didn't have to use his life saving knowledge after some of the pileups for the lad on the bottom invariably came up half drowned.

Gov. Charles M. Dale and his party, which included Maj Richman Margeson and George Bridle viewed the tilt from the shelter of the press box as did May—or Mary C. Dondero during part of the proceedings.

Proceedings were considerably delayed in the second half due to the fact that it was necessary for the officials to take bearings on various objects ashore to determine the mythical location of the yard stripes when measuring for first downs.

Portsmouth High's cheerleaders, whose spirits refused to be dampened, although everything else about them was, received valiant help from a sailor who joined them, wielded the megaphone and lent much enthusiasm to the occasion. What he was doing down on the sidelines was not definitely ascertained but it was rumored he was waiting there for his ship to dock.

Eddie Anania showed a brilliant piece of quick thinking and grid strategy when he was back on safety and a Dover punt floated down to him on his own five-yard line. He let it lie at his feet momentarily until all the Dover players in the vicinity were convinced he'd decided to let them ground it rather than risk picking up such a slippery pigskin himself.

Then when they were lulled into a sense of false security he suddenly grabbed the ball and darted upfield, reaching the 18 before the startled Green players could gather their wits and stop him.

It may have been the turning point of the game, for Portsmouth, always deep in its own territory up until then, started a march on the 18 that ended only when Jim Shanley went over for the first score.

Dover rooters arrived bearing a large banner, strung between two poles, reading "Dover High School" Dejected at the outcome, they abandoned it in the stands where it was picked up and given to Assistant Coach Babe Malloy to turn over to the jubilant Clippers.

Just how many Portsmouth fans attended was not known but the "gentlemen" of the press, on the end of a line passing slowly through the bottleneck of the General Sullivan toll house, were told that 250 cars had passed homeward in the line ahead of them.

Portsmouth's harried and rain-soaked

gridiron warriors had to come home for a hot bath. The hot water heating plant at the University went on the fritz yesterday afternoon and mechanics could not get the parts to repair it. Coach Jim Culberson told his kids to dry off as best they could and hurry back to the junior high for a warm shower.

The accompanying *Portsmouth Herald* photo captions read:

Ramming through the Dover line—Halfback Jim Shanley of the Portsmouth High Clippers on his way for a 10-yard gain in the second quarter of the game in Lewis Stadium, Durham, yesterday. Jim is about to run into the arms of Billy Keays, Dover halfback, while three other Green Wave players chase him as though he were a Thanksgiving turkey. Jimmy has already outdistanced Pat Jannelle (57), Jim Tsimikles (68) and Carl Stone (61), all three are Dover linemen.

Dover smashes Clipper Stone Wall—Billy Keays, Dover high quarterback tries to sneak through the Portsmouth line but Jack Weston and Ronnie Pecunies said, "NO! You aren't going anywhere, brother." They all went down in a heap and started blowing bubbles in the nearest puddle.

PART II

Launch

CHAPTER 5

In the Navy

I joined the Navy on June 28, 1946, and was discharged on May 1, 1948. I remember the day I enlisted. Before I left, three or four of us rented a cabin in Alton Bay. All of a sudden the war in Europe was over; it was the only news. Remember the famous picture of the sailor kissing the nurse? Everyone felt like that.

The war was over, but all boys were being drafted. I had gone to the draft board on January 26 of that year; I had turned eighteen and they were looking for cannon fodder. I wasn't drafted out of school, but I was brought up for the physical. They injected me and I passed out on the floor. I told the guy "I'm not going in the Army. I'm going in the Navy." Whatever machinations happened, I don't know, but I did get my choice.

After the big game, I was ready to leave school, but I was forced to stay in class and to graduate because my father was adamant. I graduated, and family lore is that I enlisted and Mayor Mary Dondero—the first female mayor we had—came to the house to say goodbye to me, as she did to all the boys going to war. The military vehicle drove up in front of 279 and there was a malfunction in the engine or something; I stayed home that day. The next day the Mayor came back and kissed me again, and then they were able to transport me to the railroad station. I went directly to the Bainbridge, Maryland Naval Station and stayed there through boot camp.

I got a hell of an education in Catholic school, but we didn't have connections, so I enlisted. My rival, Dickie Delamura, who I fought it out with through grammar school, had a father who was a big guy at the Portsmouth Naval Shipyard. In school we'd been equals, but I enlisted while Dickie went to Annapolis and became an admiral. That's how it worked back then, probably now too.

I became a designated sharpshooter at boot camp. They decided then that sailors should carry rifles and eventually bayonets. Don't ask me why. As a teenager, I had that rifle with the scope underneath, a .22 tube feeder. In the Navy, they gave us a bolt action of some form, but otherwise they're all the same. One day we all marched down to the rifle range. They lined us up and handed me a rifle with bullets. They flashed up the targets and then there was a yell, "FIRE!" I pulverized the target, but I fired a second or two before the call and so a siren went off.

"Who fired first?" was yelled.

Up went my hand, and we all marched back across the grounds to the barracks. The chief boatswain's mate was a nice guy but pretended he was tough. He gave me a bar of heavy duty soap as punishment, and my job was to wash all the urinals with him supervising.

For obvious reasons, you were supposed to be able to swim to make it into the Navy, but I never learned how. Down I went with the boatswain's mate and stood on the end of an Olympic-sized-pool.

"Dive in," he said.

I dove in and sank to the bottom but then walked the length of the pool. I kicked my legs on the bottom and popped up a few times for air, but I made it to the other side. It was good enough. As I've said, I still can't swim. My kids swim like fish, but I still can't.

Other than in swimming, I decided to fight to get the highest mark in my unit, not just in shooting, and I did. That gets you noticed, for better or worse. So when I came on board the heavy cruiser, the Captain had been warned in advance there was a boot camp winner coming aboard—my reputation preceded me. He wanted me to have opportunity (without my knowing it); I guess in the back of his mind he was going to groom me. I'm a seaman and he's the Captain, but he took a shine to me. He had already found out about my mouth and made me his "talker." He didn't talk directly to the men; he had me to talk to all ship departments by intercom. The ship was the USS *Macon* CA-132 (132 was the ship number.) There were 857 sailors and thirty-five officers. I was just hunky Jim, an enlisted kid of eighteen, but being on the bridge all the time, I got the attention of the senior staff. On the *Macon*, I was there eight hours every day on the bridge as we would ply the North Atlantic—bumpty bumpty bump . . .

I had the top bunk on my cruiser, and there wasn't much room. There was never any animosity among the men due to my being the captain's talker. Other things, like hygiene, were more important. Showers in the Navy were essential. Cleanliness was paramount in such cramped spaces.

After my eight-hour tour as his talker, the Captain assigned me to be in charge of a section of ship stores. Part of taking care of ship stores was providing for the sick bay, ordering supplies, and making sure they were all stocked. As usual, the personality trait of my family for meticulous bookkeeping was helpful in this job.

It was told to me that our Captain was a graduate of the US Naval Academy. He subsequently graduated from medical school and worked his way up the ranks to four stripes. As the captain of a battleship, you had to have a proven record, but I learned the only medical operation he could perform was male circumcision. I noticed at the beginning of my tenure as book-keeper that every time I checked on supplies, sick bay was full of my shipmates. Some of them had legitimate medical problems, but one way out of a duty was to pretend you were sick so the ship's doctor would put you in sick bay, and it was full of malin-gerers. When the Captain heard about sick bay always being full, he went down and examined the sailors there, circumcising some of them. Sick bay became less popular after that. All of a sudden, there were 857 men on the ship and nobody left in sick bay. No one ever went to sick bay again unless they were dying, maybe not even then!

The Captain knew I had been raised strictly in the Catholic faith, but said he'd never met a Roman Catholic who hadn't ever slept with a woman and had no "experience," of which I didn't. He said to his fellow officers after maybe six months, "We have to do something about this guy." The Captain and the officers on the bridge weren't used to guys so innocent and decided to fix that. They paired me up on shore patrol with a senior non-com. I was fiercely dressed up when over the side we went, down the gangplank, and climbed in the front of a small boat headed for the Norfolk, Virginia, harbor. No one said anything as we walked up the street to all the whorehouses. The boatswain leading me was all dressed up in his spats, "Billy Club" and stripes. I wore my white sailor suit, spats and "Billy Club."

The first brothel we entered, the madam came down the stairs and sat next to me on my left. She tousled my hair. She was mid-40s to 50 and had on a full gown, black and white, and some kind of bonnet. I had a head of red hair then, and she fingered it and said, "You're cute!" Obviously, the boatswain with me had a lot of experience. He laid out the shore patrol rules for me:

"Once an hour, you take your Billy club and bang on the stairs as you go up. That tells everyone a shore patrolman is here." Clearly the point wasn't to catch anybody, just to hurry them along. So up the stairs I went, banging away. "The other rule is that if one of the men or women come crashing through the door, your job is to separate them."

The first night was calm—I banged loud enough not to have to separate anybody, as instructed, and eventually we went back to our flop house "hotel." I don't know how many bordellos we visited that first night, but we stayed the eight hours because I remember there were no fights.

The government gave those of us on shore patrol four dollars for food and a flophouse. The flophouse had a single iron bed with two pillows, an ungodly mattress, and a single white sheet. We went to bed and had to share it. It was a depressing room with a tub in the bathroom. We just piled in; we were so tired. Shortly after we arrived, there was a knock at the door and in came one of the prostitutes. At the end of the bed, she took all her clothes off and dropped them on the floor. She was a knockout. I had never seen a woman undress before, and I was in shock. She climbed in the bed, and she and my boatswain got romantic right there on the bed next to me.

After they finished their encounter, she picked up her clothes, took a bath, dressed, fixed herself up in front of me, and put her clothes back on. She reached for the door handle, turned around to the two of us and said, "See you again!"

Back we went to the ship, and the guys could not wait for the non-com to bring me back. I knew nothing about anything, and they were just waiting to hear all about it. They never asked me anything, but the boatswain filled them in on the country boy. They had a ball behind my back, I guess. This kind of thing went on everywhere we traveled. The Captain and his officer staff were enjoying having a hunky around, but I didn't realize it.

We went to Philadelphia, New York . . . we'd go through this performance at every port we went. We were still only getting four dollars per day. I imagine the pay is still next to nothing for the enlisted guys, no matter now we're spending trillions overseas.

Eventually, it was my experience as a shore patrolman in the Navy that led me to understand my grandfather's life as a policeman, patrolling the bordellos of Portsmouth. All the years my grandfather and I lived together, he never told me what his role was; I had to find out later for myself.

My mother wrote to me all the time and saved every letter I wrote to her from the Navy. What my future wife Joanne saved, I don't know. We had little personal space on board. I once received in a letter from my mother a five-dollar-bill. The pay in the Navy was fifty-four dollars per month for a plain seaman and on shore leave I learned to pinch every penny. I would not even spend money for a trolley car. We'd get off the boat and get by as best we could. I would walk back to the ship as far as I could, and thumb.

Every time we hit port, I would hitchhike home to Portsmouth, and my father would take me back to the railroad station in Portsmouth. I'd get on the Sunday night train from North Station in Boston and was able to go from North Station to wherever I needed to return to the ship. I would come home even if I got shore leave on Saturday. Generally, they let me off at 4:00 p.m. on Friday, and I had to be back Monday at 8 a.m. The Captain relied on me as his talker, so I couldn't be late. One time the train from Portsmouth to Boston was late, so I stood Captain's Mast, which is like church confession but in front of the Captain instead of a priest.

—

Being in charge of "ship stores" consisted of keeping track of everything on the ship, like being a quarter master. I never had a stripe at that time; I was a seaman, but I went everywhere on the ship, not just the bridge. The officers' mess was a room where they dined three times a day and had all these people starched and waiting on them. After the Spanish/American war, the Navy signed up a lot of Filipinos as stewards. Black sailors would work in the kitchens, too. I don't know if they let the Filipinos become sailors, but they had their own rooms and waited on the officers. I had charge of the food supplies, dishes, and cutlery, so I could see them all.

The officers lived like kings—teacups, the whole nine yards. At the same time, the food we got as enlisted men was so bad I lost twenty pounds in the two years I was in the Navy. Our food was indescribably awful; I weighed 125 pounds when I joined the Navy and 107 when I came out. We never had money to buy anything. It's still the same for enlisted men, I have no doubt.

It was the same way with our clothes—the officers were all fantastically dressed, and we had pea coats. It was horrible in the North Sea. You had to dress in the whites, a Navy enlisted uniform, but you never had any decent clothing. All the officers had wolverine coats and jackets, and all I ever had was a white hat, white cotton whites, and a pea coat. It could be freezing, even on the bridge.

Racial relations weren't very good in the Navy either. In boot camp, we had to have our teeth examined. As a child, my parents lugged me to the dentist all the time and the drilling was brutal, but because of all the dental work done in my childhood, I never had a problem later on. When you lived in my generation and had little money, you lost some teeth. I don't think we knew how to eat right. We did the best we could but had a lot of teeth rot. In boot camp, if you were black and had a toothache, you'd be in for it. If the dentist was a southerner and a black sailor had rotten teeth, they would be screaming from the drilling.

At the time I enlisted in the U.S. Navy, two or three Portsmouth High School classmates also enlisted. We ended up on different ships. When in port we sometimes visited each other's ships. I found they had great food on their ships, but not on mine. To prove my food on the *Macon* was awful, I'll mention that while at sea one of the duties of the Executive Officer on the bridge was to try the food on the aluminum tray we crew were offered. He preferred to throw the food over the side.

We would often have gunnery practice when targets would be towed miles from the ship. I vividly remember one day when I had been taught to coordinate the dials in the panel that controlled the five big guns. When all was supposedly in synchronization the gunnery officer would call "Fire." Practice was often stopped as we obviously missed the targets, and the shells either fell in the ocean or hit an uninhabited island.

Totally unforgettable was what happened to a sailor pal. When a shell jammed on the way to be fired, he stuck his head into the barrel to see the problem. At that moment the shell came loose taking my pal's head off. I still vividly remember.

I continued working on the bridge as the Captain's talker, and when there was a Mardi Gras in New Orleans, it was decided politically that they needed a battleship in port. We were moving up the Mississippi to the Port of New Orleans and the Captain was giving orders for me to repeat to the boiler room. I know truthfully that I repeated the orders as they were given to me, but somehow the whole thing got screwed up. The battleship veered off course and crashed into a cement dock. People saw it coming and scattered. The visit was a big deal—this was a show with all 850 crew members on deck—and the ship went off course because the wrong orders were given to the boiler room. Running a battleship is far from easy. Even if we were going only two knots, there was momentum: Crash! There were thousands of people for Mardi Gras on the dock watching. It was all civilians and we went right into the dock. Everyone dispersed and it was a nightmare situation. The fiasco appeared in the New Orleans *Picayune*, though I never saw the article. To the best of my knowledge, thankfully, no one was injured.

Some of the officers wanted to blame me for giving the wrong orders from the Captain to our executive officer. Initially I did get blamed, but whichever officer had messed up, he owned up to the fact that it wasn't me. It was settled on the bridge that day that it wasn't my fault. They exonerated me not out of friendship, but out of integrity and honesty. They could have laid it off on me—the low man on the totem pole (imagine the commotion on the bridge while I'm in my rinky-dink pea coat), but it didn't happen. It was a good lesson.

We anchored there eventually and got shore leave in New Orleans. I remember that vividly. I had never been to anything like the Mardi Gras. I went to all the street parades and shows—everything that Mardi Gras symbolized. For an eighteen-year-old, it was exciting!

Being Catholic wasn't a problem in New Orleans, but that wasn't true everywhere. A sailor pal of mine and I me were on shore leave in Norfolk and got picked up by two girls. They threw us in their car—a sailor's dream come true—and drove us way out in the country to one of the girl's farm. It was a hell of a ride on a dirt road getting there. The father was kind enough to put us in a first-floor bedroom, and he sent the girls to the second floor. The father was very gracious; he didn't ask us many questions and gave both of us amenities. He was kind to put us up and put up with us. The girls tried to scamper down all night, and he would immediately catch and send them back up.

After breakfast the next morning, we piled back into the car. We were happily riding along when I asked the girl driving to stop at Catholic church. Once she heard "Catholic," she slammed on the breaks and ordered us, "OPEN THE DOOR AND GET OUT!" They drove off in a cloud of dust, and we had no idea whatsoever where we were. We walked for miles, and no one would pick us up. Somehow, we got back downtown. We finally found a Catholic church, but obviously had missed Mass. We didn't have any money for the bus and had a hell of a time getting back to the ship.

At the end of World War II, a lot of troops were still in Europe. We were one of the ships sent to Europe to bring the wounded and any survivors back. The first time, we went and got the wounded. It was a mob scene; it was stretcher after stretcher getting them on. I saw streams of wounded entering the ship. We were very careful with them and gave them a lot of space, or as much as we could. The crew was 850 men on one boat. It was a big ship, but it was cheek to jowl with all the wounded on board. Once in the US, we got them to hospitals and then turned around and went back to pick up the non-wounded who were being demobilized.

On the second trip, I had an altercation with a man going home. When disembarking at the port of entry, one of the soldiers we were driving home stole my ditty bag. I caught him in the corridor and whacked him good to get it back. It's amazing what some people will do.

Cuba (Guantanamo)

For shore leave, we would anchor off the Cuban coast. The captain would give shore leave, depending on the rotation. We would take everyone ashore and there was nothing to do but drink beer and swim. The sailors would get so drunk they would fall off the docks. We'd then fish them out of the water and on returning to the ship, drag them up the gangplank. It was a ritual. There were those who drank reasonably and those who got loaded.

Puerto Rico

Puerto Ricans are US citizens. They all have different views obviously, but most must have been happy the US won the Spanish-American war and freed them from the oppressiveness of the Spanish government—they were bastards! To give the crew of the heavy cruiser shore leave, we got to stop in this fascinating territory and to visit San Juan.

On shore leave we would walk all over San Juan, which is simply beautiful. I only saw the streets, buildings and what I could see walking on the ramparts, which was the old city mostly. I spent a lot of time walking the walls. It's just gorgeous! We were roaming around, and I had my first introduction to a bottle of beer. My favorite shipmates and I went to what we called "sleaze bag bars," cantinas, dumps. Our pay was very little. I had never drunk alcohol, and we went to have a beer.

Prostitution was everywhere. One of our shipmates had a proclivity for casual female encounters and picked up a prostitute. They were in the men's room when the door suddenly flew open with him against it. Apparently she had just coldcocked him! Here was this skinny little skinny guy hanging onto the door, which she stepped out to leave him. I suppose we lugged him back to the ship eventually. He later found out she had infected him with gonorrhea and he ended up in sick bay—with the same result as the others: snip, snip!

Panama and Argentina

Perón came to power in Argentina when I was in the Navy. I remember there was some problem with the Argentine Navy, and whether it was over the Falkland Islands (like when the whole British Navy was patrolling Argentina) or something else, I don't know. We were sent down during one of the days we were patrolling Panama and sailed along the Argentinian coast. I think they were sending a message to Argentina. There had to have been some political situation, but as an enlisted man, you never really know.

In Panama, we were on the Atlantic and the Pacific sides, going through the Panama Canal. We went on shore leave there and roamed around Panama City, which is full of colonial architecture. I've always enjoyed architecture and was amazed. Four of us hopped from bar to bar. One pal even climbed a telephone pole to the very top and hung on the top rung spread eagle. We were all aghast of the gravity; he could have touched a hot wire, and you can imagine the wiring in Panama. He climbed back down and lived that day, but not for very long.

When the heavy cruiser anchored at a munitions dock, one-by-one the sailors carried aboard the eight-inch shells and stored them in the munitions department. Since the Captain decided that firing cannons would be another endeavor he'd add to my education, he instructed me to go into one of the eight-inch turrets. I sat in a pivot chair and was told what to do. There was a big steel wall with all kinds of unfamiliar dials. (I have never been very mechanical and to this day, can hardly turn on a TV properly!) I was told after careful instruction to coordinate upon eventual orders from the gunnery officers and to be prepared to fire the eight-inch battery.

Subsequently on a Caribbean trip, I was put in the eight-inch turret after a U.S. destroyer towed a target miles to the rear. The executive officer basically said, "Prepare to fire," and I did the best I could with all the dials. The eight-inch battery in my charge fired and monstrous shells flew out. We missed the target completely, and the shells ended up on an abandoned island. I did the best I could but was never put back there again.

The same guy that climbed the telephone pole, who I really liked, was on deck one day when there was a malfunction—a shell jammed in one of the guns. My friend was investigating the reason why the shell hadn't arrived when it suddenly showed up and took his head off. It was an indescribably horrible experience having my friend die right in front of me in the gun turret.

Reflections on the Military

From the day I went in the Navy, I realized there was always someone I had to take orders from and absolutely obey. I have no regrets. In fact, if I had my way, everybody would spend two years in military service. The lessons learned from serving my country will stay with me forever.

One time, traveling on the train from Portsmouth to North Station to board the USS *Macon* CA-132 docked in Philadelphia, I was a little late because I'd walked from the station to save money rather than ride the trolley. The next morning at 8:00, I was sent to the Captain's mast along with anyone else who had committed a minor infraction. Each man was asked why he was there, or the officer would ask, "Were you late yesterday?" I would answer honestly, since it was everything my family taught—to tell the truth. There was no punishment, and I don't know if it was because I told the truth or because the infraction was so small.

The final touching story of my career with the Captain was the day I went down the gangplank for the last time. By that time, I may have had two stripes—seaman second class—and had been with him for two years. When I was in line, he came down and whispered to me, "Seaman Shanley, I'll get you a third stripe if you stay with me." I was sort of a humble boy, but I was ready to go and said, "I appreciate it, Captain, but I'm going home to college."

CHAPTER 6

A Big Shot . . . But Not Yet

When I got out of the Navy, I was required to go someplace for three or four days of rehabilitation or reintegration, whatever they called it. You had to do meager work at the homes of officers such as cut lawns, etc. I still had my brains, so it was annoying to have to do this. I realized I still had no status and decided to do something about my future.

When I was completely discharged, I used some of the money from my last paycheck and traveled, for once, without hitchhiking. I came back to 279 Wibird Street in Portsmouth.

I wanted to go to college, and a football scholarship had always been my plan. At the time, Boston University (BU) stuck in my mind because they were the only people that recruited in our local high school at that time.

Because of my ability as a football player in high school and being the fastest on the team as a "safety," my father took me to Buff Donelli, the head coach at BU, for an interview. As I mentioned before, I had lost a lot of weight in the Navy—the food was so bad!—and came out weighing 107 pounds. Donelli was up front and told me he'd let me try out but needed me to understand I was extremely "light." He told me it would be difficult living in the dormitory, and I would have to get on a trolley car to the practice field with my uniform. He also pointed out that I had the ability to go to college with the GI Bill, so I didn't need a football scholarship. He was absolutely right.

My father and I thought maybe I could lug my uniform onto the trolley, but it was very short lived idea because I was just too small. Even the uniform was impossible—I wouldn't have my mother to clean it for me. Nothing would frighten me—I was like the main character in the movie *Rudy*—but it was an impossible situation. My idol was "Harry" (Aristotle George) Agganis, the famous football player for BU. He had a bullet pass and was called the "Golden Greek." I never played on the team, but I did go to all the games, and he was Mr. All America—an all-star.

I started at BU as quickly as possible when the GI Bill was in its infancy. I lived in a freshman dorm with a guy from Maine. The proctor was also from Maine, and I had the bedroom adjacent to him with my roomie.

My parents never had money to give me, so I worked and saved before and during college. I lived with my parents the first summer at BU and continued my romance with Joanne. I had all sorts of menial jobs; for one, I dug ditches with a shovel. There was a bridge being built between Hampton and Salisbury, and after work, the foreman would take me to what was truly a fleabag hotel for a drink. He was known everywhere for the number of beers he could chug, but I was smart enough in those days never to get loaded.

So I was out of the Navy, home from school, and digging ditches. I went to get a haircut from the father of my closest pal, Alphonse Cabrera, and sitting in the other barbershop chair is a scout looking for characters for a movie. After I left, the scout asked Mr. C., "Who's the kid with the brick-red hair?" He gave the scout my phone number, and he called my mother to ask if I wanted to be a movie star. He said I would be working for Louis de Rochemont, who was famous for directing movies, especially the short news reels shown before feature films. It sounded better than ditch digging, so I signed up.

The first shoot was in Portland, Maine, and my job was to slug a payroll manager when he came out of the bank and steal his loot. Mr. de Rochemont sat in a leather director's chair wearing spats and tight pants—the whole costume. He said, "Mr. Shanley, I want you to really slug him!" We went on rehearsing two or three scenes, but he didn't like what he saw. He finally yelled, "This is the last time I'm telling you!" So I wound up and slugged the actor, just like he told me. I had one single pair of decent pants, which I happened to wear that day, and I ruined them wrestling the guy on the pavement. They reimbursed me for the pants, though, and the scene made the cut. Citizens were gathered around when out of nowhere came running the proctor from BU, who asked me, "What the hell are you doing here?" I explained that I was now a movie actor. Beans they paid me, really.

For another scene, they took me to the Dover, New Hampshire, jail. My character had been arrested and was going to be electrocuted. They slit my pants (again!) and had prepared me for electrocution. A priest with rosary beads was taking me to the electric chair, and the scene closes as the door opens. The movie was a short called *A Day with the FBI*. The only time we ever saw it, Joanne and I went to Pawtucket, Rhode Island. We rode down on the train at great financial sacrifice. I'm told it's on the Internet now for free.

My first wife, Joanne, was my high school sweetheart who waited for me to return from the Navy. I know people have said, "Why would this beautiful girl be interested in a red-headed shrimp?" Her mother was Mary Murphy, which made Joanne half Irish, so maybe that had something to do with it. Her father, Dr. Lawrence Hazzard, was a superb golfer, and he and my future brother-in-law introduced me to the sport. My future wife was the youngest of his children and the apple of his eye. She grew up at 303 Miller Avenue in Portsmouth, and after her parents divorced, Dr. Hazzard would pull up in front of 303 and loudly toot his horn. Of course, she would dutifully run out to see him. Though Joanie always cared for me, it was obvious throughout my relationship with her father that he didn't consider me up to the standards he would've liked for his baby. Still, our romance survived through high school, the Navy, and our college years.

Joanne and I were married before I had graduated from college. After our honeymoon, we drove down to Providence, Rhode Island and rented a one-bedroom apartment. I took the bus daily to the railroad station and would ride the train to Boston. I couldn't afford to take a cab, so I'd walk from North Station to BU. Joanie waitressed and also worked in Lynn teaching speech therapy while I attended Boston University. We eventually ended up living in another one-bedroom apartment in Allston, Massachusetts while I went to law school. I'd again ride the train to North Station and go through the same performance. I still use my briefcase from those days.

After law school, I came back to Portsmouth and worked for Attorney Charles Griffin. He and his partners were all very kind to me. I worked for fifty bucks a week, and by this time, my son Joseph had been born. Joanne and I lived with my moth-er-in-law, whose brother Bob was married to my pal Dorothy Emery. I owned one suit and one dress shirt, and my wife or mother-in-law and wife would wash my shirt every day. I walked from Miller Avenue to the law firm on State Street every day.

When Joanne and I moved out of her childhood home, the

only place we could find to rent was a now-condemned shack at the end of Fish & Game Road in Greenland, N.H., which was a dirt road off Greenland Road. Everybody hunted in Greenland, so guys would be out by our clothesline in their hunting gear. I probably weighed a whopping 115 pounds by then, but I could have killed them. "We've got a baby here for cripes' sake. Scram!"

When I worked as a law clerk for Charlie Griffin, one of his friends and clients was Mr. Arthur Cook. He was elderly, quiet, and needed an assistant auctioneer, so Mr. Griffin told me to apply. I suppose with my personality and charismatic approach to things, he thought I'd be a good candidate. I never shut up! I worked with Mr. Cook and we sold everything—cutlery and coin collections, furniture, and on and on. I learned a lot, and my sales pitching abilities may have been what gave him the idea to later help me change the course of my life.

After the first six months at the law firm, Mr. Griffin raised my pay to seventy-five dollars. I was a paralegal drafting his briefs and studying to take the bar exam. He trusted me and gave me all the material I needed to write a brief in defense of certain county commissioner. I was barely out of law school, and my brief helped the New Hampshire Supreme Court to exonerate him.

Things were finally looking up! I proved I could do the work and was looking forward to becoming a partner in the firm, with all the rights and privileges thereof.

I then proceeded to fail the bar exam.

That was it. Attorney Griffin ceremoniously handed me a key and said, "John O'Leary and I own a house on Marcy Street. We think you'd make a better real estate broker than lawyer." The idea was, since I wouldn't be in the law office anymore, they were giving me a chance to sell real estate. He had expected me to become a partner, but gave me a key and that was the end. I wasn't exactly fired, just . . . transferred out to begin a new career.

It was a killer for my mother and father when I flunked the bar. If it wasn't for the GI Bill opening the housing market for first-time buyers, I might not have had a prayer. I was living in a virtually condemned shack in Greenland with a wife who was now a full-time mother. My only potential income was one house to sell, so I scraped together an advertising budget of thirty-five cents a day. I put three black-and-white lines in the newspaper and kept an eye out for other work.

Later, we moved to a duplex in Newfields, one house up from the railroad tracks. In the other half of the house lived a guy who ran the kitchen at Simplex Wire and Cable. I told him about my predicament, and he offered me a job with him. He sensed I had brains, so he put me on the counter after working in the kitchen awhile. The men would line up for their meals.

A guy I went to high school with came through the line every day. The first time he came through and saw me, we were back to my Irish problem. He wanted to make sure I knew he had a job for Simplex while I—formerly first or second in our high school class—was working in the kitchen, so he flipped me a dime. I wanted to punch him! I supposed the coin flip symbolized to him his own superiority. To me it symbolized ten cents, so I put it in my pocket.

CHAPTER 7

A Little Shot at Last!

*"You're not a big shot, you're a little shot," my
wife tells me. "A little-shot millionaire!"*

W hen I first started out selling houses, I still didn't have a car.
I'd walk up Fish & Game Road in Greenland, thumb a ride into
Portsmouth, and stand in front of the North Church to meet
clients.

Couples would drive up and ask, "Why are you getting into
our car?"

"Mine's in the garage," I'd tell them.

Despite everything, I decided to take a gamble and make
a go of the real estate business. It was post-World War II, and
I was an agent on the cusp of a building boom. There were no
licensing requirements at the time, and the profession was a
den of unbelievable people. I was totally unaware of what I was
getting into—a lamb among wolves.

Simultaneously, I had a job in York, Maine, as a clerk in a
men's and ladies' clothing store. I would ride a bus from Portsmouth to York with a very nice lady. The store was owned by a
couple, and the husband would travel by train to Boston each
week to buy merchandise. His wife would close the store some

afternoons and invite me to her apartment. She was a knockout, but I carefully avoided that situation!

In one of the adjacent run-down hotels in York were women who were obviously prostitutes. They would come into the store throwing their bosoms and bottoms around, and I was selling like crazy. I was their audience while they ran in and out of the changing rooms. When husbands and wives or boyfriends and girlfriends came to shop, I'd take down five or six shirts or sweaters and display them while matching neckties with shirts. The owners of the place couldn't believe how much I was selling, so they adopted my wife and me and took us out to dinner all summer.

Finally, I found a couple who wanted to buy Mr. Griffin's house. I knew enough from law school and the law firm that I could take them to the bank for a mortgage, so that's what I did. Just like that, I had my first commission.

Soon after this first sale, a Portsmouth chiropractor referred a friend who needed to sell his house. Somehow or other, he recommended me because of his friendship with my wife's Aunt Kitty, who told him, "Little Jimmy's in the real estate business. Call him." This is where community comes in.

It was a beautiful home on the corner of a prominent street, and I advertised it with a picture. I bought a 4'-x-8' piece of plywood at the lumberyard and had a one-eyed guy paint it. Some pals help me, and we erected it right on the corner. It was a sturdy sign. A lady climbed up on it, and we took a picture of her sitting atop the Jim Shanley sign. I was so proud of this second listing.

A couple I graduated high school with came to look at the house. He was a successful Portsmouth businessman, and he and his wife fell in love with the house. They brought their parents and everyone admired the house. I sold it for the full asking price, $16,800—a lot in those days—and the commission was $800. The parents double-backed that night and told the sellers they'd give them $16,000 and cut me out, but they were told to get lost. I probably typed a contract, but the sellers could have easily cheated me if they'd wanted to. Fortunately, they were honest people.

Down I went to the Piscataqua Savings Bank with my second sale. The same stuffed bear that was there when my mother took me as a child was still there, staring at me. The bank president, E. Curtis Matthews told to the couple's lawyer and whoever else was involved to follow him. To me, he said, "You, Shan, sit next to the bear." They marched into the conference room and had the closing without me.

I sat with the bear until the closing was over. Hours passed, and the women in the bank pulled down the shades at closing time. I finally spoke up, "I'm here to receive my commission." The banker and I had a confrontation, but he finally went to the teller and got the commission for me. One of the president's assistants, who lived across the street and knew me well, finally handed me the $800 check. I had never seen that much money.

I was still running ads in the *Portsmouth Herald* and looking for new listings but invested the first eight hundred dollars back into my business. A GI came to me to buy a house, so we went to the same banker, who said to me, "Shan, this bank doesn't give GI loans." I told him that by law, I was allowed to present veterans to him. I said that if the bank didn't give GI loans, I could get in touch with the Veterans Administration. He knew immediately that I would, and thenceforth we developed a long-time friendship. The GI also got his home. After that, many of the GIs coming back from the war came to me to buy houses. I shoveled

GI loans through that bank, and the banker and I ended up great friends. The banker was a Yankee, naturally, and he had a rough personality, but even in the old days, he had always wanted the Irish to place money in the bank and get loans. They sure did.

I had youth, stamina and enthusiasm; and I became a skyrocket. Reputation-wise, I started getting lots of listings. I was doing the listing myself in those days and went to all the local banks. I owned no car and went to the commercial bank president to get a loan for one. He was another Yankee banker, but what a nice man. I told him I didn't have any collateral, but he was thinking, 'The McCafferys and Shanleys." My family had little money, but we had a great reputation. I told him, "I don't want to embarrass you, sir, but a Ford dealer I know has been trying to sell an ugly green car with no heater." He said I had "a lot of brass" and agreed to give me the loan, so I got the car. People say they remember me taking them around in my green, two-seater car. Later I bought a Lincoln Continental that Joanie approved.

When we moved from Greenland to 381 Middle Street in Portsmouth, I had a one-room real estate office and hired an air force officer as a salesman. As a prisoner of the Japanese in World War II, the officer came home to 381 to a woman I knew who had waited for him. She bought another house up the road and told me to sell 381, so I asked if I could buy it. I went back to the Piscataqua bank and told Mr. Matthews I wanted to buy the house for $17,500 using the GI Bill. It was a beautiful house with three floors and a gorgeous yard for the children. Suddenly, I owned this mansion with my wife and, and later, Joseph, James, Mary Jane, Brenda and Michael.

I developed a lot of listings and hired a secretary. I bought two desks in Portland and got a couple of phones. We crowded into one room, and I went around to the immediate homes on both sides on Middle Street, knocked at doors, and asked neighbors for permission to put a small sign in front of their homes stating "Shanley Real Estate." I worked my tail off.

—

I had been in the business a short time when late one evening at my home office, the doorbell rang. Two men were standing there, Mr. Erminio Ricci (the developer of Elwyn Park) along with a competing real estate agent I knew very well from childhood, Bob Simpson. Bob was an heir to Simpson Clothing in Portsmouth, and his ancestors had outfitted soldiers from the Revolutionary War. I knew Mr. Ricci as an immigrant who came to America from Italy and became a multimillionaire. I invited them in.

Bob was my competitor, but I was then just a two-man operation with a secretary. Erminio was a very brilliant human being. He asked me if I would join them as his agent to help sell the lots and future homes to be developed in Elwyn Park, where pre-sales weren't going very well. I was delighted with the opportunity.

It was the start of a long relationship with Mr. and Mrs. Ricci. Bob later became president of the Portsmouth Savings Bank. In future years, Joanne and I and he and his wife would travel together to real estate meetings.

Bob and I, with Mr. Ricci's backing and financing, sold the lots and houses. Mr. Ricci owned the land, and it was all subdivided and approved for building. I brought in my builders, and they purchased lots from Mr. Ricci. (Since day one, I have legally kept my real estate business totally separate from any partnerships.) Architect Lucien Geoffrion became the principal architect. I already had a loose, separate partnership with J. Paul

Griffin, Ferris G. Bavicchi, and Frank Costello. I gathered stock plans starting with 42' x 24' and 44' x 24' homes. I built a port-folio of plans and people picked what they liked. We graduated almost immediately to oblong 44' x 26' and then 46' x 28' due to demand. We were "selling houses like hotcakes" because we could sell anything. Mr. Ricci was initially building anything a customer wanted, but he mainly specialized in red brick homes because he had trained as a mason. (He told me when he started he was a cement "hood carrier" and helped plaster my home on Middle Street.) Elwyn Park prospered and became probably the largest single-home development in the city, even up to this time.

Then Pease Air Force Base arrived, with officers and families needing housing. They had temporary bachelors' quarters, but the married ones wanted to bring on their families. I had built a busi-ness relationship with the President of the Bank of New Hamp-shire, an older man, and I proposed to him that I would bring air force officers up to Concord, New Hampshire, for mortgages. I had a continuing friendship with him and his office. The officers came to look at Elwyn Park and thought it was great. What a great opportunity for me. The mortgage rate was low, and they were young pilots bringing up families and children. Mr. Ricci turned all his buildings and lots over to Bob and me, and my builders Fred Brown, Glen Rowlings and Oscar Lizotte kept building houses, with me acting as sole commander of my sepa-rate real estate operations.

Mr. Ricci allowed Bob and me a full real estate commission, although we always offered to co-broker with other realtors and pay an appropriate proportion of the commission to them. These were the Halcyon years in the growth of Portsmouth and in my business.

Miss Hazel Woods moved to Portsmouth and opened the

Howard Johnson restaurant at the traffic circle from I-95 into Maine. It was an immediate success. She knew Mr. Howard Johnson and purchased his name and controlled style of building and menu by franchise.

She immediately purchased from me a lovely single-family home on Woodbury Avenue in Portsmouth. We had a wonderful friendship until her passing.

Hazel decided to consider buying the Rockingham Hotel in Portsmouth. She did so and would take Joanie and me to dinner almost every Saturday night. I was never a good ballroom dancer. Hazel immediately brought into the wonderful ballroom and restaurant a black tie orchestra, and she and Joanie would put up with me doing my best dancing. It was a happy time.

As years passed, she decided to sell the hotel and asked me to represent her. When a large development company contacted her, she told them to "Call Jimmy Shanley" in no uncertain terms. That started a friendship that I treasure to this day, with attorney Terry Farrell. Up he came from Boston, along with three or four officers I knew with architect Jerry Weiss. When they purchased the Rockingham, they hired Weiss to plan the future condominiums.

When the Portsmouth Redevelopment Authority voted to bring Portsmouth from a quiet, small city into a more vibrant community, I had been in the real estate business for a few years. The board of directors of this initial development corporation was composed of almost all men of Yankee heritage. They chose to implement their ideas in the Portsmouth area known as The Orchard, which consisted of open land from Middle Road and Greenland Road to Highway 95 across the Route 1 Bypass, where the car dealers are now located. As a boy, I had walked the land with my .22 rifle, so I was intimate with the scope of it all. As it happened, the land was owned by my childhood lawn care customer, Mrs. Borthwick, my "Yankee dowager."

The group had approached Mrs. Borthwick about buying her land but was unsuccessful. The President of the Portsmouth Trust Co. (who later became a personal friend and mentor) came to my office to ask if I would be interested in joining the board. Underneath it all, they had decided they needed an Irishman and a Jew, so they also asked Harry Weinbaum, who happened to be one of my clients. (I had also played sports with his son in high school, so we had a history.) Predictably, Harry and I were put in the back when the board went to meet her, but the relationships quickly changed when she noticed me in the back and asked me to come up front and sit with her. I supposed because of our previous relationship when I was a kid doing her yard work, she knew I'd work my tail off and she could trust me, so she insisted to the board I be in charge of the development. I did not let her down. Borthwick Avenue was named for the Borthwick family. It was a dream opportunity for my real estate career and right up until her death, the beginning of another solid friendship.

—

I've always been persnickety about appearances. This was helpful when I decided to commission a company logo. For the company logo, I picked the colors myself—the Shanley color was plum. Naturally, it couldn't just be one color; it was a mixture of three.

For a logo, I wanted the best. I asked myself, "Who is a brilliant graphic designer?" I found Charlie Conn, a designer involved as an instructor at the Massachusetts College of Art. He introduced me to the school's President, William "Bill" Hannon, and they did the logo for me. The three of us have remained close friends over the years.

After our meetings over golf, introducing our wives, and getting to know each other, they decided there was something I could do for them also. They believed that information about what it was going to be like going out into the world as fledgling graphic designers was missing from the curriculum for their graduating classes. They wanted the students to learn how to take an interview with the hopes of getting a job or commission. We set up a role play where I would be the embodiment of a tough employer. I would go once a week and set up a series of lectures, and they would tell me how they would approach me as a possible employer. I did the best I could with it. It was interesting for them to pretend they were coming for an interview and see how I viewed the business world.

Business Culture

Reputation is everything in business. I had a dozen partners in various ventures and always kept anything with the Shanley name 100% under my control. If anyone turned out to be a little sleazy, the arrangement ended.

My team was very strong because all the players exhibited integrity and truthfulness. We had twelve offices—from Kennebunkport beyond Northwood—and our signs were everywhere.-We had tremendous co-brokerage as well. We began having quarterly parties for teambuilding. The cooperation and teamwork was fun, but it was also symbolic. Our parties bound our offices over all the years.

Marie and I had a Royal Barry Wills design home with two acres and a big backyard, so I would have a circus tent put up for a summer party. In the winter, I would hire a first-class comedian from Boston for that party. I also knew a man with a yacht, and he generously allowed us to use it for another of our parties. For Shanley Day one year, we got permission to hold our party at the Governor Benning Wentworth historical home.

The concept of "Shanley Shillings" was created by my wife Marie. For every sale an agent made, they received Shanley Shillings, which were similar to poker chips. Each person's sale was valued, and they would get shillings as credit. The company had an annual poker night, for which I'd rent a small ballroom. Marie would purchase exquisite gifts, including trips. The staff would bid on the items, and a lawyer or judge I had invited would act as auctioneer. Those who had a lot of shillings would share them behind my back. We called it "the shifting of the Shanley Shillings," and it was riotious.

Everyone would be present, from here to Timbuctoo. It was exhausting giving so many parties, but I had a lot more energy than I have today. Marie would get tired of my antics, but I called it teambuilding.

The Jim Shanley International Golf Tournament

I have been golfing for sixty years, seventeen of which I sponsored the Jim Shanley Invitational Golf Tournament. It started out as a one-day golf tournament for either twelve or sixteen players, all friends of mine, and grew into much larger affairs. The idea got started when I played golf at The Country Club in Brookline, Massachusetts.

The Country Club was the bastion of "only Yankees could belong." But they decided in the mid-sixties to bring over a famous Irish pro, and a pal of his was my friend James Weldon. The pro invited James to bring friends to the club, and he invited me, Ferris G. Bavicchi, and Joe Gaulen. The four of us arrived at the club and were introduced to the pro. We went into the clubhouse and here we were—an Italian, a Frenchman and two Irishmen. We took the entry stairs and went into the locker room. They had an attendant, and we did the best we could to act like the gentlemen we were.

Leverett Saltonstall was a famous Massachusetts Senator. As we played, he came down the sixth-hole fairway and gave us the fish eye. He looked at us like, "Who are these guys?" We were breaking the code by being permitted to play golf. After eighteen holes, they brought a cart out, away from the clubhouse, with whatever we wanted to drink, but we were never permitted in the clubhouse area. Having been used to the hierarchy in Portsmouth, it was a poignant moment in my career. My enthusiasm for the Shanley golf tournaments started right there in Brookline. Years later, we had one of the tournaments at this club.

Marie and I would meet people all over the world when we traveled to play golf. On two occasions, we met golfers who eventually joined the JSIGT. I used to hire professional comedians from Boston to entertain while Marie and the sales office staff organized everything else. For the first one, a chef from the Wentworth came to cook for us. He got bombed and fell into the fireplace. A lot of men got loaded and slept all over the place. It started out with twelve guys and mushroomed into forty-eight over the last few years. I had a penchant for inviting a lot of rich men, but I had many golfing friends of modest means that would come also. After Marie and I were in Morocco and met Dr. Billy Dang, he would fly here to play in the tournament too. It became a very important social, male affair. The women complained sometimes, especially when it went from one day to three. You wouldn't believe how many wives would chase me down trying to find their husbands. It was uproarious. Marie could tell stories about that! We were invited to Concord Country Club one year and played eighteen holes before returning to my cottage on Pleasant Lake in Deerfield, N.H. The chef from the hotel again came to Deerfield and prepared a wonderful meal in the lower level, fire-placed room.

We had a total of seventeen tournaments at country clubs all over New England and drove to every one of them. They were held at Cocheco (NH), Concord (NH), Portsmouth (NH), Manchester (NH), Ferncroft (MA) Brookline (MA) Arundell (MA), Portland (ME), Hartford (CT), Bald Peak (NH), Balsam Hotel (NH), Mt. Washington (NH), Woodstock (VT), Abenaki (NH), Blue Hill (MA), Dover (NH), and the Wentworth Golf & Tennis Club (NH).

—

How did my real estate career end? I was downtown Portsmouth in Market Square one day and told a psychologist friend that I was coming apart at the seams. He set me up with a psychiatrist in Boston, and after two years of weekly sessions, he told me, "You are going to have a heart attack and die."

I closed my company the next day and sold every piece of real estate I owned except my personal homes. I had thirty-five successful years in the real estate business and have been happily retired for over twenty-seven years now.

PART III

F AMILY T IES

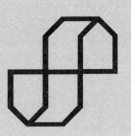

CHAPTER 8

Joanne

My first wife was gorgeous and a loving mother. She passed away in 2002, and I am including this short history out of respect for her and our family.

We started dating in high school. She was a knockout while I had freckles and lots of red hair. She was a real Portsmouth High School beauty. Though I was a football star, everyone wondered why someone who was sought after by every boy would want to go with me.

She was the Hazzard family baby, and her father idolized her. My father-in-law and I were both very proud of her, but he never really liked me. Underneath it all, I always knew he didn't think I was good enough for his daughter. I did, however, become good friends with Joanne's brother-in-law, Bob Heltzel. He and Dr. Hazzard introduced me to golf, so Joanne bought a second-hand set of golf clubs for me. Her father was a superb golfer, and he loved to beat the hell out of me in golf. It was hard to intimidate me, but I was subservient to him because I loved Joanne. He kept me in my place.

Joanne was an equestrian and was in riding shows with Sylvie, her beautiful silver riding horse. I was so proud of her ability! I went to the farm in Rye where Sylvie was boarded and tried to learn but was never a good rider. Joanie's step-mother was

so jealous of her that after we were married, she got her husband
to sell the horse rather than to spend money to board it. Joanne
and I drove all over New England tracking her horse but never
found it. It was a very sad ending and a crusher for Joanne.

After I got out of the Navy, we got married as quickly as
we could. We had our reception at the Wentworth Hotel paid
for by Dr. Hazzard, who also loaned us one of his automobiles
for our honeymoon. We honeymooned at the Balsams Hotel in
the White Mountains, and it was lovely. Years later, Bob, his wife
Jane (Joanne's sister), Joanne and I went to New York and danced
with the Guy Lombardo Orchestra, but the first time we ever saw
one of Lombardo's bands was on our honeymoon.

Joanie's father was born in Kansas and his brother Clyde was
super-successful in farming there. Clyde had piles of money and
always wanted to buy jewels and beautiful clothing for his wife,
Aunt Ora, but she wouldn't let him. They would come to New
Hampshire for vacations and I remember dining with her; she
would have the most frugal meal. Family lore was that whenever
her husband tried to buy her something, her immediate expres-
sion was "Don't need it!" This response became a Shanley family
saying and still is today.

Joanne was a caring, fantastic mother, and the children
and I loved her. We have nothing but fond memories of her.
When the children were young, my wife and I would take them
to Rosa's Restaurant in Portsmouth. Ralph Rosa and his head
waitress, Margie, always waited on us. He had a great head
chef; everyone was crazy about his salad dressing recipe. During
the chef's lifetime he would never give out the recipe, but the
restaurant's manager one time gave me a quart as a gift. I had
a brand-new Cadillac and put the dressing beside me while
driving. Someone backed into me and the salad dressing spilled

all over my front seat. Needless to say, it ruined the seat and carpet.

One day I came home to find an elderly woman sitting with my wife on our couch. Joanne introduced me to the woman, "Aunt Annie," who had been institutionalized since she was seventeen. Joanne moved her into the house, which delighted the children. She was a little old lady in her eighties, and my daughters gave up their bedrooms for her. She became part of the family, and we included her in everything.

Joanne and I would have all sorts of couples over for dinner with the family, and Aunt Annie always sat with us. She had a trick, and the kids would signal her to perform it: take her false teeth out with just her tongue. The kids would egg her on during dinner parties, and she would twirl her teeth in the front of her mouth to entertain them. During the holidays, we would deliver a case of wine to the nuns at a school in Dover, and the Mother Superior enjoyed Annie's special talent. She ended up a gentle soul after being a violent youngster.

Aunt Annie had to be moved out of the house after a while because the children were growing up. I went to Mother Superior, who was running a convalescent home, and she agreed to take Annie in.

My children loved their mother and always took excellent care of her. My son Michael called me recently and told me "There's something we have never spoken about but that I would like to get off my mind. I want you to know that my brothers and sisters and I have always been grateful and will never forget how you were always taking care of us and Mom. You couldn't live at home, but you had caregivers for all of us. The important thing was that you looked out for all of us."

That call meant everything to me!

Obituary of Joanne Shanley

From the *Portsmouth Herald*, August 10, 2002:

RYE—Joanne S. (Hazzard) Shanley, 74, of 795 Washington Road, died Thursday Aug. 8, 2002, at the home of her daughter, Mary Jane Keane, surrounded by her family and her beloved dogs.

Born April 16, 1928, in Portsmouth, she was the daughter of Dr. Lawrence R. and Mary S. (Murphy) Hazzard. She was a lifelong resident of Portsmouth.

Mrs. Shanley graduated from Emerson College, Boston, and worked as a speech pathologist.

She was a poet who delighted in the interplay of spirituality, the human quest for meaning and the ironies of life.

Survivors include her brother, Dr. Lawrence R. Hazzard, Jr. of York, Maine; her children, Joseph J. Shanley of Portsmouth, James G. Shanley of Newburyport, Mass., Mary Jane Keane of Stratham, Brenda C. Shanley of Salem, Mass., and Michael C. Shanley of Hilton Head, S.C.; five grandchildren; and several nieces and nephews.

Addendum:

SHANLEY—Joanne S. (Hazzard) Shanley, 74, of Rye, died Aug. 8, 2002. Her family respectfully honors her wish to have a private family celebration of her life. In lieu of flowers, memorials may be made to Rockingham VNA and Hospice, 137 Epping Road, Exeter, NH 03833, or to the

NHSPCA, 104 Portsmouth Ave., Stratham, NH 03885. Arrangements by the Farrell Funeral Home, 684 State St., Portsmouth.

CHAPTER 9

Fatherhood

All my children have a different personality. Dramatically different.

I worked seven days and nights a week when they were young and my real estate business was booming. I would pick up prospective clients in my car to look at homes, but when any of my children had an after-school athletic practice, I'd make the potential buyer come with me to watch them. They weren't amused, but years later would razz me about it. I made a lot of good friends this way.

We also didn't have time for vacations except to our summer home on Pleasant Lake. I saw it advertised in the *Portsmouth Herald* and took my partners in the Danbury Corporation—Dan Reagan the electrician and Andy Fabrizio the plumbing contractor—on my first visit. I fell in love with it and paid the full asking price. Buying a lake house was one of my best moves. It was a ritual to go up there every summer.

I then bought a fantastic Chris Craft speedboat and drove it with instructions. All of my children became expert water skiers and were trained to swim at the Wentworth Hotel pool. The kids stayed there every summer with their mother, and I would go up at night. Pleasant Lake was a pure lake and still has beautiful, mountain-fed water. We built a great dock, and the lower level had a brick fireplace. We fixed it up quite a bit. It was wonderful.

Next to us at the lake was a retired U.S. Marine Corps senior master sergeant who lived there with his wife and daughter and also had a speed boat. His daughter was friends with both my daughters, and she eventually moved to Rye. Another cottage was held by the McCourt family, who had seven children. Our family still tells fun, fascinating stories about them. All the families and children at the lake were close.

I paid $13,500 for the lake house and sold it for $125,000. I've regretted selling many times, but what happens in families is once kids start to get married, a place like that leads to stress. "Harry" or "Suzy" wants it for the month of July, and suddenly you start having strife over whose turn it is. That was the main reason I sold it, before there were any problems. We all cry about it, but I either had to sell it or buy five more.

I lugged them everywhere. I once took them to Canada skiing—I spent my life tying their boots on skis. The kids all play golf a bit, and the boys went to the Shanley golf tournaments. We were just a happy family, as I was in my family, always to be that way.

With my successful career in real estate, my children never had to go without money when they were young. They had what I think everybody would like to have, but it never spoiled them. They never had to worry financially, but they have not ever asked for anything—they don't give a rat's ass about my money. Maybe they'll throw a party with my pile if I don't blow it all before I die. It would be a great time.

Joseph John

Joseph was the first child, born on Memorial Day, May 30, 1953. I vividly remember bringing him home from the hospital. He was so small I could hold him in the palm of my hand and dance with him. At his birth, Joanie and I lived at 303 Miller Avenue in Portsmouth with her mother. It was usually just the three of us, but there was an aunt that would bomb in and out (Aunt Kitty). Joanne's brother would come down and do his business on the phone in the hall, too.

My business started taking off soon after Joe was born. A lady friend who owned 381 Middle Street (I met her when I was a letter carrier to the house during World War II) decided to put her house up for sale when her husband was released from a POW camp in Japan. I went to the Piscataqua Savings Bank and asked Mr. Matthews for a mortgage. He granted it, and Joanne and I moved into 381 with Joseph. Then the children began arriving . . .

Starting with Joseph, the children all went to St. Patrick's School for nine years. He then went to Portsmouth High School while his four siblings went to St. Thomas Aquinas. Joe was a superstar at PHS—fullback on offense and linebacker on defense. The team was so successful that in his senior year, it was invited to the Shrine Game—the "Maple Sugar Bowl" they call it—and was victorious over the Vermont team. He was more interested in girls and sports than anything else; women flocked to him as he had charm. I never missed a game. I have wonderful memories.

In the summers during high school, Joseph and his younger brother James had their own painting business. They were both natural entrepreneurs. I never helped them paint—I have no painting ability—but like to think they learned the lesson from my cornball stories, the example being the 13 grass-cutting jobs, blah, blah, blah. Since they performed well, they developed an innate sense of running a business. They bought their business equipment from their own earnings. If ever they needed money, I supplied it.

Joseph matriculated to Deerfield Academy, playing football. It was as ritzy as you could get, and he was a star there, too. He met people like Lily Pulitzer's son; a typical Shanley, he always seemed to gravitate to people who are fascinating. Joanne and I attended games at Deerfield Academy whenever we could, and I clearly remember traveling to New Jersey for one.

He and James and I went on extensive college interviews. I had been making some money, so I could afford to let them pick a school they wanted. They both picked Lehigh University in Lehigh, Pennsylvania. They both joined fraternities, and Joseph was a wild man.

Joe came back to Portsmouth, got his real estate license and went to work with me for eight years. He saw my whirlwind lifestyle and wanted to join. I got to mentor him, and we were always very close—for those eight years, I saw Joseph every day. When I retired, he would come through my front door each day in the late afternoon just like I went to my mother's house at four p.m whenever I was in town. He would come through the front door at 10 Harborview and yell "Dad!" and we would just chat. We would occasionally go on a jaunt to play tennis or golf. He went to all the Jim Shanley International Golf Tournaments and would also fly down to Hilton Head, South Carolina. It was a wonderful relationship, and we retained it all the years until his passing at fifty-nine.

I gave him the hardest job in my organization—managing the commercial department. He immediately proved himself as a salesman. I was building everything except skyscrapers, and he was also in charge of property management—the worst job of all. Property management is a difficult profession. It involves managing homes, apartments and commercial leases, and he had to rent buildings or sometimes sell them. Other times he sold businesses. He got very involved.

Joseph had studied business in college and would often go with me on listings so we could discuss how we were going to approach handling either a lease or sale of a property or building and meet the client. We were together all the time. We had lunch almost every day, played tennis or golf, dined, and drank. He had a pile of friends, and I kept an eye on him. We were inseparable.

When Marie came to work for me, and before she took over the sale of the condominiums at the Hotel Rockingham, she invited Joseph and me to dinner one evening. He and I came in separate cars, and there was a small cliff behind my real estate office in Kittery, Maine. It was late at night, rainy, and there was a small curve. When I hit the brakes, my car went over the cliff to the right. Unfortunately, Joseph immediately followed me over the cliff and we landed side by side. We got out of our cars and crawled up the banking, which was covered with thorns. We arrived at the top bloody and were greeted by the local police, who immediately said the Maine State Police were on their way. The Kittery police drove us home. The front page of the next day's *Portsmouth Herald* read, "Son Follows Father."

My business style was tumultuous with many offices, and Joe had been building up a fascination for charitable work with Big Brothers/Big Sisters. Another organization he supported is called "A Safe Place" which helps women whose husbands are abusive. As the years went by, I remembered his wife telling me about a call he got from a woman at a pay phone in Rochester. He got up in the night and rescued her. He was always interested in charitable endeavors.

When Joseph came into the business, our office was at 22-26 Market Square. I had two private secretaries and six real estate salespeople. It was luxurious. On the left as we entered the building was the waiting room, and on the right was the real estate sales manager's office. In the center was a beautiful entrance hall where the office secretary sat. The interior was Carrara marble from Italy, brought over on a boat. We were so proud of our office! It is now occupied by Rí Rá, an Irish pub.

On the first floor were safety deposit box rooms on both sides. There was a staircase leading to my office and another large office at the end of the second floor. I bought the space previously housing the First National Bank of Portsmouth and turned it into our commercial department. Joseph had an office and a waiting room there with four salespeople. Walking up the stairs, we had to go through the former Portsmouth Trust boardroom, which we turned into a conference room.

Joseph put up with me for years, but he was more interested in do-good-erisms. He was not solely interested in making money. He finally came to me and said that, with all the offices and people, he felt it wasn't for him anymore. He had had enough of the tumultuous lifestyle I was conducting in my business and was interested in having his own company. He asked me, if I were starting over, what would I do? I told him he should have a boutique real estate company so he could earn a living at the business he liked—real estate sales—and have a small staff, which he did immediately. He took on everything! He was successful but never had more than eight salespeople, which was the maximum he wanted.

Joe's career was in real estate, but he had an avid interest in charitable work. He was "Mr. Portsmouth." He was an auctioneer and real estate agent who raised millions for charity—he was obsessive about it all his life. I was a capable auctioneer, but never as ruthless as Joe Shanley. At his auctions, he'd pick people out of the audience to harass. He'd go from table to table and raise hundreds of thousands for non-profit organizations. He was a combination comedian and auctioneer. He'd be coached about certain people and just go around the room torturing them to raise money. Part of the draw was to see Joe perform.

Joe died on November 28, 2012, at fifty-nine years old. His death prompted a memorial with over 1,000 attendees at the Wentworth by the Sea Hotel as reported by the police.

James Garrison

Like all the kids, James went to St. Patrick's School. He then followed his brother, Joseph, with whom he had the painting business, to Portsmouth High School and Lehigh University. He graduated from Northeastern University after spending two years there.

James met his future wife at the New England School of Photography in downtown Kenmore Square, Boston. He is a talented photographic artist with a good "eye," and he had perfected his photography. He spent some time taking pictures of skyscrapers and other commercial properties for contractors. His wife was a graphic artist with great ability. They rented quarters in a building in Amesbury, Massachusetts and began a printing company called B. Designs, Inc., where they created specialty paper items using their artistic abilities. They are both now retired from B. Designs and on to future endeavors.

James got deeply involved in Newburyport, Massachusetts politics, and his sister Mary Jane ran his campaign for mayor. He was defeated by a local female attorney and has been on various governor-appointed boards in Massachusetts. (Like James, I only ran once for political office and lost.)

I have the pleasure of his company practically every week,

and because I'm no longer driving, he takes me to the men's club.

Brenda Carol

She was adorable. Both she and Mary Jane! She was born in Portsmouth and attended St. Patrick's School for nine years and was the brightest of the bright. She will hate for me to be talking about this, but she is a real genius! She attended St. Thomas Aquinas High School in Dover, Lesley College in Boston, and then Graduate School at Harvard College where she received a master degree in education.

Also while at Harvard, she met John Strucker and they subsequently married. He was an adult literacy teacher and later an educational researcher at Harvard and is now a consultant. He is a bright guy, and they are very happy together. Brenda teaches middle school in North Andover, Massachusetts, and is very happy about her career choice.

Brenda is an attentive daughter and spends time challenging me to be the best person I can be. Brenda and John have perfected their golf games in recent years while enjoying summertime golf outings.

Mary Jane

My daughter Mary Jane has a heart of gold. She, too, was born in Portsmouth and went to St. Patrick's School then St. Thomas Aquinas. She graduated from the College of New Rochelle in New York and stayed there to receive her Master in Education. After graduate school, she ran an after-school program at the Boys & Girls Club of Boston. She came to work with me as a real estate salesperson at 22-26 Market Square on a commission basis. She is a real spitfire, super successful, and a very good golfer. She is now an incorporator for Piscataqua Savings Bank.

Mary Jane has become a very good golfer. She fell in love with Thomas Keane, a prominent Portsmouth lawyer, and married him. Tom and Mary Jane have four sons: Jonathan and Matthew (from Tom's previous marriage), and Kevin and Thomas. They raised them in Stratham with a pool and a lot of acreage. My grandsons are very successful in their individual careers.

In 2005, Mary Jane became heavily involved in founding Womenade of Stratham, which now has nine chapters in New Hampshire. Womenade was founded on the principle that there are a lot of families in need of help. Its mission is to provide short-term financial assistance to its neighbors in need. The group raises money doing various things, and everyone is a volunteer. Mary Jane plays a very low-key role, and I never found out about her involvement until the beginning of 2014. It fills me with pride to see my children involved in worthy projects like this.

My children have all been very attentive to me, and I've been attentive to them.

Michael Conrad

Michael attended St. Patrick's School, Berwick Academy, Cardigan Mountain School, and Brewster Academy in Wolfeboro. He received his diploma from St. Thomas Aquinas. With his personality, my son Michael would have been dynamite as a Realtor. He actually spent two years selling real estate, but not for one of my companies. He later sold cars for a living and is now a very successful antique dealer, which requires real people skills. He definitely inherited the ability to articulate.

Until Michael came along, I never had any difficulty with any of the kids. I run a tight ship. He was a handsome boy and always a little full of it. He came to all my golf tournaments, and women were always noticing him. It's been that way all his life.

The best story I tell about him is when he went to private school at Cardigan Mountain in Hanover, New Hampshire. Marie and I would visit him, and we went one weekend to pick him up. This was part of my fatherly approach to make sure everything was going okay. At the Dartmouth Inn for dinner, we were passing by the bar to get to the dining room when the lady bartender said, "Hey, Mike, good to see you!"

I said, "Mike, what's going on?"

He said, "Get with it, Dad. My friend and I climb out the window at school sometimes and have a few pops at the Inn."

I'm his father, but I'm a prehistoric square, and he was obviously very socially successful.

After graduation, he flew to Hawaii because Joanne's brother, Bobby Hazzard, had a plumbing company there. Bobby was working everywhere on the Hawaiian Islands and had television ads that said, "If you can see Mauna Kea [the big mountain there], we're available." He took Michael on as an apprentice plumber for two years.

When Marie and I were on Kauai, Bobby and his mother, sister, and girlfriend made the trip from "the big island," Hawaii, by motor launch. We had a wonderful time, and they departed the next day.

Michael was a very interesting boy. He is now successfully running a massive store called Michael & Co. selling antiques and furniture restorations on Hilton Head Island. He lives in a magnificent home in a lovely subdivision with his wife, Luba, and the story of how they met is quite interesting. Marie and I were at home in California and went to an amphitheater in San Diego where a couple of Russian guys brought over two different troupes of trapeze artists. We watched these magnificent young people performing, while at the same time in Savannah, Georgia, Michael saw the second show. It turns out the two Russian guys had a scam going and took off with the dough. They left these helpless Russian boys on both coasts with no money. Michael took in at least five, and other people housed some too. He got involved with the Russian legation in Washington, DC, and they got them back to Russia. The boys invited Michael to come visit their country, where he then met Luba. They had a whirlwind romance, like something out of a storybook, and he flew her over to Hilton Head. They were married there on the beach. They have been together three years now and are very happy. Luba was a seamstress for the Russian officer corps, so Michael got her all the equipment she needed—sewing machines and the whole nine yards. None of the women in the area had anything like it, and she was slammed once the word got around. She did everything and could work seven days a week. I'm very proud of her, and of him.

Christopher

Michael was my last child, and Christopher was his twin. It's a sad tale for us, as Christopher died at birth. The undertaker, John Farrell, and I drove to Calvary Cemetery the day before Christmas to bury him. Christopher was on my lap in a small casket on the way. The grave digger had dug a small grave through the thick, frozen ground, and I buried him myself with John and the grave digger's help.

We said prayers and goodbye. Father McDonough told his mother, "Christopher is in heaven with the Lord."

Grandchildren

My grandchildren call me Grampa Jim. They are all very successful, too. I saw my grandkids all the time while they were growing up.

My one granddaughter, Tristan Pappas Shanley, is Joseph's daughter. She married Michael Riestenberg from Minnesota, and they moved to Albuquerque, New Mexico. When her father died suddenly, she moved back to Portsmouth immediately to take care of her mother. It was a very difficult time. She is the business development officer for the Provident Bank.

Years ago, I sold homes in Pannaway Manor in Portsmouth for between ten and fifteen thousand dollars. Tristan placed a bid on one of these homes next to Pease Air Force Base. She came bursting into the house one day and said, "Grandpa, I bought a house!" She had colored pictures and was very excited to tell me about it. The sale never actually went through, but she did find a house adjacent to Elwyn Park.

Both grandsons—Kevin and Thomas—are Mary Jane's and Tommy's. My information is that they are in Alaska right now jumping out of helicopters to ski. I am not surprised since they have been rambunctious since forever. "Dad, could you come out and babysit?" Mary Jane would ask me. Once the little devils hid on me, and I couldn't find them. They thought it was a great game! I called Marie and she came charging out. We had a hell of a time finding them. They roar about it today.

Kevin went to the University of Connecticut. He is a superb athlete and became an expert skier. He was captain of his college's ski team, and after college the people at Jackson Hole, Wyoming, immediately hired him. He works with the ski team in a coaching position. Kevin became fascinated with river rafting out there, too, where he conducts tours of the Snake River and Yellowstone National Park. He is a superb golfer and could always (like his dad) beat the tar out of me.

During college, Thomas had an opportunity to intern with Flatbread pizza. One thing led to another, and Thomas was running all over New England with the company. Currently, he's working with Flatbread in their corporate development department. Thomas lives on the Seacoast enjoying all that New Hampshire offers young people who surf and ski in their free time.

Reflections on the Tribe

Upon reflection, I had nothing but love from aunts and uncles and my parents, who obviously adored me. I know my own children knew they were loved and cared for. As they grew, I would take them to Boston. I remember an experience with James at the Christian Science Church. He went up in the belfry where the organ was and hid. I found him and gave him a lecture. Corporal punishment was not my style; nor was it a style in my family. I raised them with love and caring . . . and long lectures.

Joanne was a fantastic mother and didn't have to work because I made enough money, and I would have a lady come in to help her. In years following, the same woman would take care of the children while Joanne was hospitalized at various times. She would cover for me when I went to visit Joanie or take her to appointments. As is evidenced with the story of when Michael's call, my love of Joanie and her love of me permeated our marriage and the raising of our children.

I don't think they ever had to worry about any gossip about their father and mother; they lived with praise of them. People loved Joanne; they loved me. There were the few in town, especially the Irish, who may have talked behind our backs, but not many.

When my kids were at St. Patrick's and the weather was good, they would run up to my mother's house after school to get cookies and converse with their grandmother. My mother was so proud of them; she just adored my kids. All holidays and birthdays the family got together, especially Christmas, with the big tree in the bay window of 381. All the presents would be hidden in the attic, and we would bring them down on Christmas Eve. They never told us, but all five kids would go up there to inspect their gifts and see if they got what was on their lists.

Love and caring and teaching—with me, I honestly think my children emulated the relationship I had with my parents, something I'd say we can all be glad of.

I always knew the value of family and of staying close, even today.

Tributes to Joe Shanley

It's expected for a father to brag on his children. In Joseph's case there were a lot of other people who took the time to remember him, and I think it's worth including those words here, too.

From the *Portsmouth Herald*, November 28, 2012:
"Shanley was not your average Joe"
By Charles McMahon

PORTSMOUTH—The city has lost perhaps its best sense of humor. Well-known businessman Joe Shanley died Wednesday morning at age 59.

The owner of Shanley Realtors since 1988, Shanley was also a beloved husband, father, broker and auctioneer, as well as a good friend of the community.

Shanley's brother-in-law, Tom Keane, confirmed his passing Wednesday afternoon, saying the death was sudden.

"The community has lost a really fantastic guy," Keane said.

As a boy, Shanley attended Saint Patrick School, a small Catholic school on Austin Street. He attended high school at St. Thomas Aquinas in Dover and then went on to Lehigh University and the University of New Hampshire.

Shanley's professional resume included being past president of the New Hampshire Realtors Association, director of the Northern New England Real Estate Network and member of the New Hampshire Commercial Investments Board of Realtors. He was also a past member of the Big

Brothers/Big Sisters board of directors.

Having worked with Shanley since 2000, fellow Realtor Dave Lefebvre said his colleague had perhaps the most energy of anyone he knew.

"He gathered the energy from people he worked around and shared it," he said. "His means of doing business was to focus on results with integrity and excellence. That never wavered."

Lefebvre said he'd always admired Shanley for his dedication to his profession. "He loved what he did," he said. "He was damn good at it, too."

Shanley also applied his auctioneering skills to numerous local nonprofits in need of a financial boost.

Over the years, he routinely entertained at benefit events held by the Special Olympics, Cystic Fibrosis, Cross Roads House homeless shelter, New Hampshire Association of Realtors, Strawbery Banke Museum, Foundation for Seacoast Health, City Year New Hampshire, the local school system and many other charities and private clients.

In 2008, Shanley was recognized by Friends Forever as the inaugural recipient of the Eileen Foley Award, an award presented to citizens who have helped make the world a better place.

Stephen Martineau, executive director of Friends Forever, said Shanley's passing saddened the organization and affected him personally.

"Today is one of the saddest days for Friends

Forever and me personally," Martineau said. "Joe's humor, honesty, thoughtfulness and, above all, compassion elevated all those who knew him, be it kids from either side of the wall in Belfast or community leaders in Portsmouth. He was truly a one-of-a-kind friend, and words cannot adequately convey our sorrow at his passing."

Shanley was also a past recipient of the "Spirit of the Seacoast" award and was named a Paul Harris Fellow by the Portsmouth Rotary Club.

Rotary President Nancy Notis said Shanley was the epitome of the organization's mission, "service above self."

"He was truly one of a kind," she said. "There will never be another Joe Shanley."

In addition to his distinguished career in the local business community, as well as his dedication to various Seacoast charities and nonprofits, Shanley was perhaps most renowned for his ability to make people laugh.

Having traveled in many of the same circles as Shanley over the years, City Attorney Robert Sullivan said he considered his friend to have a true gift of wit.

"It was the quintessential Irish-Catholic ability to see humor in nearly anything and to make others see it as well," Sullivan said. "However, there was an understanding and intelligence behind the humor that was remarkable."

Sullivan said it was Shanley's humor that

made him an institution in the city and helped him earn an opportunity to open for renowned comic and Academy Award winner Steven Wright at The Music Hall.

Local attorney Peter Loughlin agreed with Sullivan, saying Shanley's sense of comedy was unique all to itself. Loughlin said he considered not only Shanley's wit to be irreplaceable, but also his commitment to the community to be unparalleled.

"He was larger than life," Loughlin said.

Longtime friend and former city mayor Tom Ferrini said in addition to having the "best sense of humor imaginable," Shanley had a mammoth heart.

"Joe was the kind of guy that would give you the shirt off his back," Ferrini said.

Obituary of Joseph J. Shanley

From the *Portsmouth Herald*, November 30, 2012:

Joseph J. Shanley

PORTSMOUTH—Joseph John Shanley, 59, died Wednesday, Nov. 28, 2012. Joe was born on May 30, 1953, in Boston, Mass. He was the son of James and Joanne Shanley. He was married to his loving wife, Cindi, for 33 years and had one daughter, Tristan, who recently married Michael Riestenberg.

Joe attended Saint Patrick School of Portsmouth, where he was the favorite pet of the Sisters. At Saint Thomas Aquinas High School of Dover, Joe, a diligent student, found time to become a star athlete and make the 1971 N.H. All-State football team. Joe attended Lehigh University and the University of New Hampshire. At Lehigh, he was famous for his acerbic wit and creative antics. His tenure as fraternity social chairman was legendary.

Joe was the owner of Shanley Realtors and Auctioneers, LLC and was a very active member of the Seacoast community. He was past president of the New Hampshire Realtors Association, director of the Northern New England Real Estate Network, and member of the New Hampshire Commercial Investment Board of Realtors. He was the inaugural recipient of the Eileen D. Foley award for World Peace issued by Friends Forever. Joe was also the recipient of the Spirit of Seacoast Volunteer Award in 2007-2008 and received the Paul E. Harris Award from the Portsmouth Rotary Club.

As master of ceremonies at the Annual Friends Forever St. Patrick's Day Roast, Joe's gifts of humor and storytelling were on full display. He was the highlight of the evening. Joe's sense of humor and quick wit were his stock in trade. He was the opening act for celebrated comedian Steven Wright at the Music Hall for the benefit of Cross Roads House. With his auctioneering talents, Joe raised millions of dollars in support of local agencies. Among them are The Foundation for Seacoast Health, City Year, Special Olympics, Big Brothers/Big Sisters, Cystic Fibrosis Foundation, New Generation, Inc., UNH Athletics, American Heart Association, Portsmouth Lions Club, Portsmouth New Hampshire School System, and Friends Forever. For over thirty years, Joe gave generously to a multitude of nonprofit organizations.

Joe is the son of James A. Shanley and the late Joanne Hazzard Shanley. He is survived by his wife Cindi, whom he adored, and his daughter Tristan, the light of his life, and her husband Michael Riestenberg; his stepmother, Marie Downing; his brother James and wife Karen Battles; sister Mary Jane Keane and husband Thomas and their four children Jonathan, Matthew, Kevin and Thomas; sister Brenda and husband John Strucker; brother Michael and wife Luba Afanasyeva; his brother-in-law, Scott Pappas and children Megan and Missy; his sister-in-law, Kassha St. Jean and husband John and children Nicholas, Ashley and Taylor; and his beloved aunts, Mary Ellen Serino and Martha Shanley Hass.

SERVICES: The family extends its invitation to attend a celebration of Joe's life at 10 a.m. on Dec. 8 at the Wentworth by the Sea Hotel, New Castle, N.H. In lieu of flowers, please donate in Joe's memory to any of the above mentioned charities.

"Blackjack"

My grandfather

Me and my grandmother

My grandfather, parents and me

OLDEST AND YOUNGEST

These officers are said to be the youngest and oldest policemen in New Hampshire. They are Paul Connors, 24, left, and James A. McCaffrey, 72, both members of the Portsmouth department.

James Andrew McCaffery on the right

My dad, Joe, in 1915

Mom, Aunt Ali Lyons, Aunt Connie, Uncle Freddy and Dad

Me and my father on Wibird Street

My mother and I

Baby Jimmy

Me on a rented pony

My first bike

Me in my knickers

Wibird Street Shanley Gang

My Boy Scout Troop #158

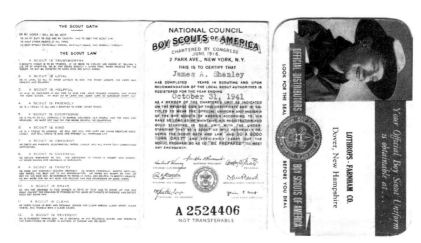

My Boy Scout Membership Card

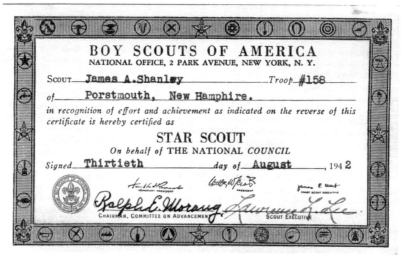

My Star Scout Award 1942

138

Charles Doleac, Sanford Sherman, me, Carl Morin, and Gregory Whalen

Shanley Real Estate ad in Portsmouth Herald

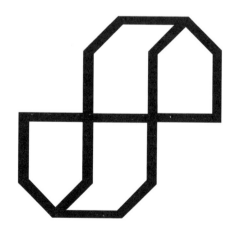

Shanley Real Estate Logo

140

My first real estate sign

JIM SHANLEY AGENCY, INC. OPENS KITTERY BRANCH OFFICE

Jim Shanley, president of Jim Shanley Agency, Inc., Realtors with offices in Portsmouth and Deerfield, N.H. announces the opening of their newest branch office at 17 Whipple Road, Kittery, Maine. Shown at the recent opening are left, Kay Power, branch manager, and right, Jim Shanley. The new office will serve Kittery, Eliot and York and offers complete Real Estate Services including sales, rentals, rental management and appraisals, and is a member of The Seacoast Multiple Listing Service.   adv.

Kay Power and me

My football days

PHS Football Team, 1945 State Champions

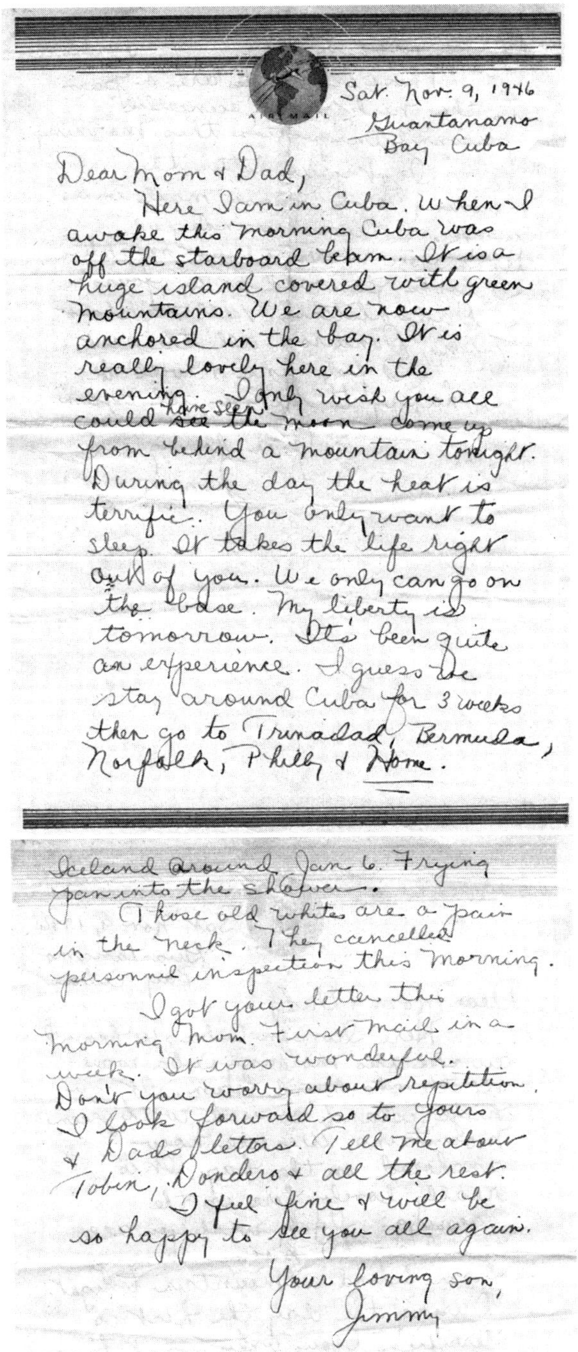

Sat. Nov. 9, 1946
Guantanamo
Bay Cuba

Dear Mom & Dad,

Here I am in Cuba. When I awoke this morning Cuba was off the starboard beam. It is a huge island covered with green mountains. We are now anchored in the bay. It is really lovely here in the evening. I only wish you all could see the moon come up from behind a mountain tonight. During the day the heat is terrific. You only want to sleep. It takes the life right out of you. We only can go on the base. My liberty is tomorrow. It's been quite an experience. I guess we stay around Cuba for 3 weeks then go to Trinidad, Bermuda, Norfolk, Philly & Home.

Iceland around Jan 6. Frying pan into the shower.

Those old whites are a pain in the neck. They cancelled personnel inspection this morning.

I got your letter this morning mom. First mail in a week. It was wonderful. Don't you worry about reputation. I look forward so to yours & Dads letters. Tell me about Tobin, Dondero & all the rest. I feel fine & will be so happy to see you all again.

Your loving son,
Jimmy

Letter to Mom and Dad from U.S. Macon

James Weldon, Ferris Bavicchi, Joe Gaulen and me

381 Middle Street, Portsmouth during bicentennial celebration parade in 1975 headed by Prince Charles

My first wife, Joanne, at Wallis Sands, 1945

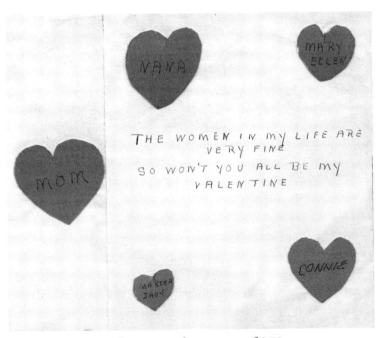

Valentine to the women of 279

Joanne and I on our wedding day

Joanne Scofield Hazzard

146

Joanne's and my five children

Uncle Freddy & Aunt Connie at 279 Wibird Street

Aunt Connie with Freddy

Uncle Freddy, Aunt Connie and their son, Frederick

Aunt Connie dancing with Freddy

Uncle Freddy

My son, Joseph

Joe receiving the Eileen Foley Award

My son, James

My daughter, Mary Jane

My daughter, Brenda Carol

How to get that job

Knowing what the hurdles are and how to clear them

by Duke Richard

Even before she applied for the job, 25-year-old Brenda Shanley knew she had two major hurdles to clear. First, she was changing career fields, and second, she had no real experience for the job she wanted.

But she compensated by doing several things that employment specialists strongly recommend.

Along with her neatly-typed one-page resume that briefly detailed her work experience (both paid and volunteer), she wrote a strong one-page cover letter that told her prospective employer why she thought her background made her an ideal candidate for the job.

She followed up with a telephone call, just to make sure that the proper person had received her resume and letter. At the same time, she got in a comment or two on how interested she was in the position.

This helped get her to the interview stage. Then the former junior high school teacher, who had returned to her hometown seeking a new career, prepared for the interview by intently studying the product that she would be selling if she got the job.

The position she was seeking was that of classified advertising manager for *Seacoast Woman* magazine. She saw the ad in one issue, applied, then intently read every issue she could get her hands on.

She also talked with people, like her parents, about the position and her background, to insure that it was one she really wanted.

By then she had an appointment

Brenda Shanley cleared the hurdles and got the job. (Duke Richard photo)

in the paper and thought I would apply."

Peabody also liked Shanley's apparent interest as expressed through telephone calls. Following the interview, Shanley called back to clarify a point she had tried to make so that it would not be misinterpreted. This gave her another opportunity to verbalize her interest in the position.

Shanley then had a follow-up or second interview with Peabody and her superior.

Several days later she called again to see if a decision had been made. Told no, that it would take a few more days of interviewing, she called once more.

Resource Associates is a professional and personal counseling agency.

The trio agrees on several points:

• Do your homework by learning as much as possible about the job, the company or its products before an interview.

• Accentuate the positive on your resume, during the interview and at the follow-up.

• Follow up. A telephone call or a thank-you letter following an interview makes you stand out in the crowd. Even if the position is filled by someone else, your sincerity and politeness puts your resume in the front of the files if a similar position becomes available.

able to explain their previous job responsibilities, to describe a typical day on the job, to tell what motivated them to apply for the new position and to detail specific accomplishments or problems they have dealt with in previous work experience.

He notes that work experience doesn't have to be wage-earning. Volunteerism counts, he says, especially if you can translate your experience into skills required for the job you are applying for.

Carol O'Brien of Liberty Mutual, where many positions are clerical, agrees. A complete description of duties will help downplay the volunteer aspect, she says. "We look for someone who likes to work independently at routine tasks."

Dale O'Reilly, a personnel consultant who locates people for companies, suggests contacting an agency, particularly if you are changing careers.

"If an agency says they have nothing right then, but to send a resume, do it. You never know when a company may request a person with your background."

O'Reilly recommends ways to uncover jobs: by using personal contacts—friends, relatives, anyone you associated with or meet; finding out what businesses are coming into the area—contact them before they get here and stress that you're a local person who can help them; by knowing the job referral system of a company you're interested in working for—if it posts jobs inside before looking outside to fill them, have a

Brenda in the Portsmouth Herald

My son, Michael

The Shanley Gang at Turks & Caicos in 20__

My forever pal, Alfonso (Al) Cabrera

My mentor, Bradford Kingman

154

Henry Powers   *Judge Gerald Giles*

My brother-in-law, Bob Heltzel   *My friend, Jim Tarpey*

Ferris Bavicchi, Best Man at my wedding to Marie Downing

Marie and a reporter in front of Nelson Mandela's home

Marie and I after our wedding

Meeting Secretariat

Marie reading her favorite newspaper

Me cruising

Jim at Pleasant Lake

My granddaughter, Tristan

My grandson, Thomas James Keane

My grandson, Kevin Joseph Keane

CHAPTER 10

Meeting Marie

My wife Marie calls me a "charismatic son-of-a-bitch" and a sly fox, but Napoleon himself wouldn't hold a candle to Marie—there's nothing she can't accomplish when she gets set on it. She is a walking brain, queen of the Kentucky cotillion and a Kentucky champion swimmer. As our business life went on, she was so brilliant that she taught many of the real estate classes for the company. She's indispensable in every way. She loves my kids and she's put up with me for forty-seven years.

Marie's father was a physician (he died when she was four) and her mother was a nurse, so she has always had an interest in medicine. She went to grammar school like everyone else as well as the University of Kentucky, and then Transylvania University with the bright people. She should have gone to medical school, but it's not a subject we discuss. She never had any children, and how can anyone choose to marry an Irish Catholic with five children when all these rich boys want to marry you? Lucky for me she did.

Marie was living in Portsmouth when she separated from her first husband. She chose real estate as her career and asked a local district court judge she knew for advice about where to be interviewed. He recommended two reputable firms, and fortunately for me, she picked mine. She impressed me deeply in that first interview. Unfortunately, I had no openings in the company at that time, but she had made an immediate mark.

A short time later, my client and friend Hazel Wood, the owner of the Hotel Rockingham, was approached by North American Development about buying her hotel. This provided an opportunity for Marie to manage the project, so I called her and we met at a State Street restaurant. I explained that I was heavily into a project and needed someone with ability to cope with all that was happening. I told her it was a golden opportunity if she wanted to work. She took it on and it was super-successful. (Ferris Bavicchi was instrumental in it as well.) With this success, I told Marie she had to spend some time in the trenches. She started selling real estate, became one of my top salespeople, and was the future VP of everything. I had four or six salespeople, including Marie and Gregory. I put the two of them basically in a basement closet of my second real estate office while I worked upstairs in my ceremonial office.

I got to know her, and one thing led to another. I fell madly in love! It's been forty-plus odd years since I took her to see Harry Winston, the New York jeweler—I already had expensive tastes—for a wedding ring.

I had my mother happily on my hands and saw her every day when in town, but she had no idea of my life. Somehow word got around. Mother would say, "I've heard about that Downing woman," referring to Marie. Poor Marie. She's so wonderful—she lights up for everyone. She went to see my mother on Wibird Street. Recall, my mother dominated the house. My grandmother only had to look at you, but once my grandmother got sick, my mother ruled the house by swooning. My mother went to Mass every morning, and she was a lovely, charitable lady, but when it came to Jimmy, she watched every move. When Marie went to see my mother and told her we were getting married, of course my mother swooned. Marie knew it was hopeless, but it was one time my mother wouldn't get her way, swoon or no swoon. All the same, there was no way my mother would come to our wedding in a Protestant church. My children all came, as well as many relatives and friends. Marie and my mother never met again.

Marie's mother was Mildred P. Downing of Lexington, Kentucky. Her father was from Alabama, but was originally from Chicago. Her grandfather was a full-blooded Cherokee Indian, so Marie is a quarter Cherokee. When Marie and I decided to get married, I felt I needed to meet her mother by myself. I was then and am now an old-fashioned guy. I explained I was interested in marrying her daughter.

Marie's grandmother had been something else back in the days when women weren't supposed to work outside the home. She was a big caca in a local bank, Edgar County Bank and Trust, where Marie's farms are managed today. The grandmother's husband is also a legend in the area. They had four daughters, one of which was Marie's mother. The other three were all spinsters and professors at the university. One had been an artist and worked in Italy; we have her paintings on the wall now. When I went to pledge my troth, I knew about some feelings in the south. I figured that as an Irishman and a Catholic, I could be in for a rough time. I flew down by myself, hit town, and moved in with her mother.

I had manners, so Marie's mother had to introduce me to all the aunts. I turned out to be an interesting person to them; they had not met an Irishman like me before. One of the sisters had always wanted to go to the American Legion Hall, so I took her. She enjoyed a whiskey and so did I, Johnny Walker Red. I went to visit Marie's mother because I didn't want to deceive her, so I was just being myself. Jeepers Creepers, Marie's mother was a proud member of the Lexington Country Club! She wasn't involved with Kentucky society—she WAS Kentucky society! She worked for the C. V. Whitney Farm and was the U.S. thorough-bred horse registrar. She took me to the Keeneland Racetrack; she wasn't hiding me in the bush. I was obviously successful, but even with five children and an Irish Catholic background, I suppose she knew there was no point opposing my relationship with her one daughter.

After four or five days of being nicely lugged around down there, I soon brought her mother to Rye. Later I brought some of the aunts up, too. When we eventually went to Canada, I included her mother on the trip. I've always been a conniver in a nice way and wanted to do everything I could to please Marie, as I do today. I adore Marie. Her mother wouldn't have had any choice, thank goodness.

Our wedding was a ball! I proposed to Marie that we have a big wedding, and she bit for it. With her agreement, I invited fifty couples we knew. I made hotel reservations, and there were a hundred guests from New Hampshire alone, never mind her southern relatives and friends.

Our wedding reception was at the Lexington Country Club in Kentucky. I hired a couple of buses and we visited with Secre-tariat, even though I wouldn't know the front from the back of the horse. I have a whole album of photos. We went to horse farms, and Marie's mother made arrangements at Keeneland where all the races are held. We had bands, everything! You name it; we had it. It was a four-day party with all kinds of great food and everyone thoroughly had a blast. The ceremony was performed by her mother's minister and is a treasured memory.

CHAPTER 11

Friends

Someone remarked to me recently, "It's amazing how many friends you have. No one ever leaves you—they're like barnacles to you." It's true. Here are just a few of the many people that I've grabbed onto over the years.

Alfonso "Al" Cabrera

Alphonso "Al" Cabrera lived on Marston Avenue. His father was a wild Spaniard and his mother was a sweet Canadian lady. We walked to St. Pat's School together for nine years. In eighth grade when Sister DeLords would send me home early Friday if I upset her, I would always head to Al's house. His mother would talk to me until it was safe to be seen on Wibird Street. Al and I both got our licenses at sixteen, and he was a wild driver.

His father came from a village in Spain named Rhonda. (Marie and I went there eventually to see his family home.) The village was way up in the mountains, and according to Mrs. Cabrera, Al's father as a young man went to Argentina and rode with one of the Pancho Villas in the Argentinian Army—one of the pistol-carrying revolutionaries at the time. Can you imagine growing up in this family? Al had two sisters, and we all went to school together.

Al's father had a great big black Buick, and there was a huge tree on the side of the road. Al would rev the engine and ride within inches of the tree, with me in the front seat.

We starting drinking together when he came out of the Army and I got out of the Navy. We would go out together as a team, and one night, we were in the Edwards Hotel, a terrible place in Salisbury, Massachusetts. Anyone who was wild would go to "Mushy's Bar" inside the hotel, and one night we proceeded to continue drinking there past the point of prudence. There were a couple of girls in the next booth, and though we were never good dancers, we asked them to dance. A couple of guys who took a shine to the girls asked, "Who the hell are you?" They came from Seabrook, New Hampshire, and we went out into the alley to exchange punches. I ducked from one of the guy's punches, and Al took it right in the face.

Al worked for his father as a barber, even in high school. The day after the fight, I happened to be downtown and his father asked me at the front door of the barbershop, "What happened to my son?" I told him he fell on the prongs of a bush and pierced his face. It was a cock-and-bull story, which I'm sure he knew.

While drinking at a bar in Rye, Al and I picked up a couple of girls who were interested in getting in Al's black car. The four of us piled in and drove to Odiorne Point. Nothing happened but a few kisses, but instead of driving reasonably, Al sped up on Boar's Head near Governor Spaulding's mansion. The cops pulled us over and hauled us to the Hampton Beach police station on the beach. Al was due to open the barber shop at 8 a.m. The night sergeant called us "you squirts" and made us walk along the beach the whole night to sober up before letting us go. We eventually got back to Portsmouth. Al and I had a wild youth, to say the least.

In high school, Al came to Leary Field one day to watch my

baseball game. I was at bat and Al was sitting in the stands with his legs spread. I always hit the ball as strong as I could and had a lot of agility and strength. The ball went right past the catcher and caught poor Al in the crotch. He had to be rushed to the Hospital. Naturally, I teased him for life.

He and his father worked together, and Al took over when his father got too old. He was my barber and pal forever. He was my closest friend and my best man at my first wedding. He remained my friend until his death. I had a wonderful life with Al; we shared a wonderful boyhood.

Bradford M. Kingman

Bradford M. Kingman was a native of Durham. He became President of the Portsmouth Trust Co. while I was putting a lot of real estate transactions through PTC and Piscataqua Bank. One day at my 75 Merrimac Street office, he made an appointment to come by and said the Board ("the Guys") wondered whether I'd consider becoming a Director at the PTC. There was maybe twenty years between us. We became really fast friends, as he was the epitome of "gentleman," and I looked up to a guy like that. His father was a druggist in Durham, and Brad had been the headmaster at a day school for girls in Kansas. I would talk to him about various and sundry things. I was selling a lot of real estate, and Brad was my mentor. He was proud of my reputation for honesty and integrity.

Henry Powers

Henry Powers came to me one day and said he was interested in Elwyn Park. I couldn't hammer a nail, but I had four builders. Mr. Ricci owned land on which one of the builders was building a house, and Henry liked the location. Henry was president of

Sprague Energy, whose corporate headquarters was in Maine, but they had an office in Portsmouth where he bivouacked. Sprague was owned by Axle Jordan out of Sweden. The story his wife Heppy—Hepsibah—enjoys most is that Henry and I would lunch often and order martinis with olives. These were the days when-people got away with drinking and driving. Let's just assume I was guilty and he was guilty at times. Heppy tells the story of Henry coming home loaded. She says there was a bang at the door and there I was, saying, "Let's go out some more!" and off we went. I guess you could call me the Devil. Henry and I remained friends 'til the day he died. Heppy and I still keep in touch.

Gerald Giles

Jerry Giles was a well-known lawyer in Portsmouth, and I sold him the house on Highland Street where he raised his family. He married Judy Giles, who today is a real friend to my wife, Marie. Jerry built a shopping center and massive rental space on Heritage Drive in Portsmouth. His father had a famous country store in Northwood where he bought from Canada all the pelts from trappers. I had never met anyone like his father and mother. They were Yankees beyond Yankees. It was a genuine New England country store with cracker barrels and everything.

Jerry employed me as a real estate agent. We never argued because he was the boss. He was partners with friends of mine, and we became good friends. Our best story was our junket to Belgium. Marie and I went with Jerry and Judy—the four of us off to Bruge on holiday!

I had made arrangements for a hotel there with all the amenities. We had a raucous time together. It was absolutely fabulous. Jerry was always very careful. He had family money, but they lived very reasonably, and I never did. (I've always been a spend-thrift, by my wife's standards; it was a classic clash between us.) It was the Giles' first international trip, and could you imagine traveling with me? They were rolling their eyes the whole time.

Jerry didn't take any crap from me. He kept me in line. He was not my attorney, but I always listened to him. I continued with my ways, but he would reel me in. He was a cherished friend.

Robert "Bob" Heltzel

Bob Heltzel and Mary Jane Hazzard, my first wife's sister, went together to Catholic University of America in Washington, DC, and it's where they met.

Bob was a Navy fighter pilot. His father founded Heltzel Steel in Warren, Ohio. He was maybe seven or eight years older than me. I can remember having been a little boy admiring Mary Jane's beauty, and I fondly recall her and Bob arm-in-arm coming down alumni field to watch me play football. It was like a vision: he was dressed in his Navy dress whites and she was simply gorgeous. I was on the football bench and turned—I see them in my mind right now. They had a whirlwind romance and got married.

Bob introduced me to golf. I spent a lot of time with him as an adult. Joanie and I would be with them, and he would come to 303 Miller. I remember the four of us going to NYC to a swanky nightclub. Guy Lombardo was playing, and as usual I drank too much champagne. I was violently ill in the bathroom at the hotel.

The first time we played golf, it must have been right after the Navy. Joanie visited with the golf pro at the Portsmouth Country Club and negotiated for me to own a set of second-hand golf clubs. She paid $125 for the whole kit and caboodle—bag and everything—and gave them to me as a gift. Bob was a superb golfer, and he invited me to join him at the Wentworth by the Sea golf club. Dr. Hazzard was also a great golfer. I applied to the club for a membership primarily because of his interest in the sport and Bob's willingness to teach me.

I still remember certain golf holes, but there was one in particular. On the sixth hole at the Portsmouth Country Club, I had the miraculous opportunity to have a great shot. Both Bob and Dr. Hazzard boomed it out, and although I didn't drive it as far, I hit it, competing with the doctor and Bob one-on-one. In subsequent years, I'd have less than thirty-four or thirty-five on the first nine and always wanted to break eighty, but I could never pull it off. I'd always end up with between eighty and ninety throughout my golfing career of sixty years.

I knew Bob when he was courting Mary Jane, but I remember Joanie and the doctor and I putting her on the train many times to go to the Catholic University of America. I stayed in touch with Bob forever. He was known as the "Golden Boy." He was just simply a great father. I knew all his children, and we would spend a lot of time together in Warren, Ohio. They were deeply involved with the activities of the Catholic Church. Mary Jane never stopped being pleasantly religious.

James Tarpey

Jim Tarpey was building his home in Borrego Springs, California at the same time I was building mine. We became really good friends and golfing buddies. He and his wife, Zana, golfed with Marie and me. Rams Hill was a development of eighteen holes which eventually expanded to twenty-seven. It was designed by Ted Robinson, the famous golf architect. Borrego Springs is two hours from San Diego.

Jim intrigued me. I was in California one day and we got talking about finance. He owned an insurance agency in Houston, Texas, and knew Fayez Sarafim. Somehow or other Jim even sponsored Fayez's bachelor party. Jim suggested I meet Fayez, and he invited Marie and me to go to Houston to meet him, which we did. It was a good time.

Fayez controlled the top two floors of Notable Painting. On the top floor were his offices. Jim introduced Marie to his assistant, Mrs. White, and Fayez to me. Sitting at his desk smoking a small tightly wound cigar, I immediately shook his hand and asked him if he would give me one. Henceforth for about 4 or 5 years, Fayez was a fountain of knowledge and a mentor. Marie went to Houston every year. The reason we parted was that he had assigned my file to an assistant. One day, I had a question and rather than bother Fayez, I called the assistant. He later told me that he took the call on the tarmac to get on a plane. He called me a cro magnon man and told me I was a bother. My temper got in the way of calm judgment, and I hung up on him. After having four financial advisors over the years and being a director on two bank boards, my wife and I have happily turned over our investments to a Boston-based financial advisory firm.

Ferris G Bavicchi

Ferris G. Bavicchi was my closest adult friend. He was MC at every one of my golf tournaments. He was President of Iafolla Industries. His father started it as an Italian immigrant, and they employed numerous men. They were producers of hot top, stone, and everything to do with construction. Ferris became president of Iafolla Industries in later years, as well as President of the Portsmouth Chamber of Commerce. He was a bank director and quietly into everything.

When I came out of the Navy, one of my jobs initially was at the Howard Johnson's traffic circle in Portsmouth. Ferris is the one who approached me with the "You son-of-a-bitch!" story. I would be passing out brochures in my job at the circle while he and Marga would be kissing and hugging in broad daylight in the parking area. She was one of the first to wear a mini-skirt. They subsequently married and had a little boy, but Marga later died.

He then met his second relationship, Bea. She and Ferris teamed up and were together for forty-two years. Ferris and Bea and Joanie and I were together constantly during the beginning of my real estate career. It was just a wonderful friendship. When I started the Jim Shanley International Golf Tournament, he was always master of ceremonies. We remained great friends until his death. Bea and I still keep in touch.

John "Fitzy" Fitzsimmons

John "Fitzy" Fitzsimmons was an exceptionally thin Irishman and a college pal of Paul Griffin's. Paul was in construction and hired me to be the bookkeeper on a road construction job in North-wood, New Hampshire. I worked in a barn at the end of a dirt road from Monday through Friday and would ride up in a truck with all the guys. I kept track of their hours. On Sundays, I would go and recapitulate for the payroll. I always wanted to drive one of the monster highway trucks, and one of the drivers let me! At the incline in Durham, I couldn't handle the truck and had to apply the brakes but crashed. The police came and rescued me. Paul would often bring Fitzy to Portsmouth as his guest, and he would play golf with me, Paul, Ferris and Frank Costello. He was an architect and a sweet, sweet guy. We had good times together.

Terrence Farrell

Terence Farrell is my best living friend. He was one of the members of North American Development Corp., which came to Portsmouth to buy the Rockingham Hotel. He was the real estate representative of the group and had to deal with me. Terry physically towers over me; here's this tall agent and me, the shrimp. He initially thought of me as a rube, but he soon realized I could handle him and a dozen more. He has an infectious laugh! We negotiated the sale of the hotel, which is when Marie came into my life. Through life's challenges, he has always been my friend, and I believe he knows it's the same to him and his family.

Hector Cote

Hector Cote owned a bakery in Massachusetts along with his wife and children. He was a wild man, and I was no cream puff. They were neighbors of ours at Pleasant Lake in Deerfield. During all of my first wife's illness, he was Johnny-on-the-spot at the lake to help me take care of my children. Hector was a good friend and helped me immeasurably. I couldn't have had a better friend than Hector Cote.

Frank H. McCourt

Frank H. McCourt owned another cottage at the lake and was president of John McCourt & Co., which built Logan International Airport. When his father passed away, Frank became president, and the company kept its original name. To this day, the family maintains the airport. All the kids are successful in their professions after graduating from the Catholic University of Washington, DC. My son James has retained a lifetime relationship with Attorney Terry McCourt. Frankie McCourt bought the LA Dodgers. The McCourts and the Shanleys often went to a

Chinese restaurant in Hooksett, New Hampshire, together. We would have parties at the McCourt cottage and have a taxi deliver Chinese meals to the guests. There was no end to me, even now at 86. They were a fantastic family; some of my five children and their seven children still keep in touch to this day.

Frank Jellinek

I got a call one day from the president of Erie Scientific Company, Frank H. Jellinek. He wanted to move his company to New Hampshire from Buffalo, New York. Their request was a great opportunity. His son, Frank, Jr, was integral to it all. We started out as me being the real estate agent, and I found homes for the father, son and employees. Frank and I teamed up because he was an avid golfer and his son had racing cars. I played a lot of golf with the elder Jellinek, and he had homes everywhere. Frank, Jr, bought a beautiful farm with his lovely wife and family. I had lots of happy times with both men. Frank Sr. kept a home in California also. I played golf with him in California and in New Hampshire. He was always one of the participants in the JSGT. We had a wonderful relationship.

Karen Drysdale

Anybody that can put up with me for 19-plus years . . . let's talk about Karen Drysdale. We'd all like to have a tan like hers! Karen was recommended as an office and home cleaner by my professional painter, Kate Shattuck, who was painting and wallpapering a home where Karen was gardening.

To Marie and me, Karen has become a part of our family. I even had business cards printed for her—Karen Marie Drysdale, Shanley/Downing Household Administrator. Our friends want to hire her, but she has remained in her role with us. She also works with her sister and brother, a landscape architect. I'm known to my family and friends as "the snit king," and Karen is a match for me as a "snit picker upper." She is so unbelievably meticulous that we accuse her of using Q-tips to clean any and all corners. Any specs will be "toast."

My caregivers and I decided to gather up a few "snits." We would pick strategic spots to place them before she arrived. After she finished her day's work and left, we'd march around to see if she found them, which of course she always did. Marie and I feel very fortunate to have such a trustworthy and reliable helper as a regular visitor to our home.

CHAPTER 12

Snapshots from Around the World

I have always loved to travel; I guess I caught "the bug" in the Navy. For several of my trips around the world, I traveled to places where Winston Churchill went. He would mention races in his books, and I would follow along. *Hinge of Fate* was the primary book of his I liked.

Colombia

A friend of mine had been in the construction business in Colombia, South America. He had left money in a bank down there and wanted me to have the use of it while I was visiting back in the '60s. I didn't do that, but his stories of his activity in Colombia read like in today's newspapers. Even back then, the revolutionaries were there, and I understand today they still battle.

We got off the plane as tourists with Dr. Peter Czachor (a gynecologist) and his wife Flo. We were on the bus from the airport when a group of soldiers stopped us. They were fully armed and lined all the passengers up outside the bus to search us. The bus driver came out speaking Spanish and kept using the word "Turistas! Turistas!" meaning "tourists." Apparently the country needed tourists, so they let us back on the bus. At the hotel reception desk, all the glass was bulletproof. I'd had experience dealing with the mafia in one of my transactions, so I wasn't too scared. One funny thing about Colombia was that when my wife, Joanie, and I walked the streets, the police officers and rebels knew that a lot of the terrorists would dress as nuns. In front of us, the soldiers would approach any nuns and pull up their habits to see if they had guns or knives.

Columbia is a beautiful country. The four of us have great memories from our driving and bussing around over hill and dale. The Spanish architecture is breathtaking.

Panama

I first visited Panama in the Navy. I was always adventurous. When I would get shore leave, a sailor pal—Kenny Warnock, from Boston—and I would get on a bus and head to wherever it was going, knowing it would be a round-trip. Kenny was a foot taller than me, so we made quite a pair. We would get on the bus with the natives, who carried chickens and other fowl in their baskets and on their laps. We'd ride around and have wonderful experiences, since we knew the bus would eventually come back around to the heavy cruiser. We had almost no money, but would pay next to nothing to see shows in Panama City with singers and dancers. Occasionally, we would actually hear gunfire, because the communists were trying to take over and Panama is a small country.

During subsequent shore leaves in Panama and after docking on the Atlantic side, we would go to the Pacific Ocean to visit Kenny's uncle, a civil engineer, and he would entertain us. When we got two days of shore leave, he would put us up overnight and get us transportation back to Panama City to get back on our ship. Kenny subsequently married, and whenever he and his wife came to Portsmouth, Joanie and I would entertain them, like take a trip to the Isles of Shoals and on and on.

J. Paul Griffin was one of my employers while I was in college. When his daughter went to the Catholic University of America, she met Edgar E. Ameglio Jr., the son of a famous Panamanian land owner, and they fell in love. I knew her as a young girl before she went to college. When married, they moved to Panama onto a ranch with vast acreage. Joanie and I, again along with Dr. Peter Czachor and his wife Flo, were invited by Edgar to visit. It was a very memorable trip. We landed at the airport in Panama City, and Edgar picked all four of us up in a big car. I sat in the front seat to the right of him when he got a call on some form of walkie-talkie.

It was in the days of Torrijos, the dictator. At that time, the US had a Marine detachment in an attempt to control the communist revolutionaries in the mountains of Panama. To instruct the dictator's troops, the US government sent a contingent of US Marines to train them, and we hate to admit it, but to protect the dictatorship. We didn't want communism in the western world. Edgar's father had built a golf course and was friends with the dictator. Edgar got a call on the walkie-talkie from the dictator, and Edgar called him whatever the term was for "Boss." The dictator had orders for him, but I don't speak Spanish and didn't ask for a translation. Edgar's house was interesting in that monkeys rested in the trees there. I was fascinated with them. Dr. Czachor and I played golf almost every day while visiting, and we had Panamanian men as caddies. The caddy's wives followed us, and when we'd stop, the caddies would approach their wives and get us drinks. The women carried baskets on their heads, and the men would go have lunch with them. We would wait until they finished their lunch, complete the eighteen holes, pay the caddies, and retire to the clubhouse for food and drink.

Edgar and his wife would bomb back and forth to America,

and they brought their children once they started having them. As usual I became friends with all the parties. Edgar belonged to the Panama Country Club and was part of the aristocracy. When we were down there, we were warned to bring proper garb and always to dress to the nines—Dr. Czachor and I carried white dinner jackets and bow ties without fail.

Morocco

Marie and my trips were always memorable and happy. I had always wanted to see Morocco, so we went. We went to the camel races and golfed at "Royal Golf" in the capital city.

While in North Africa with Dr. Czachor and his wife Flo, I wanted us to see the countryside, so we hired an Arab driver who called himself "Joe." Off we went with Joe driving like a wild man. We cascaded through the mountains at top speed; I was afraid we were going to go off the cliffs. I attempted to slow him down as best I could, but it didn't work.

It was a beautiful countryside, and we eventually arrived in Marrakesh. He took us to the old harem quarters there, where the pasha had kept his harem of forty women. (Can you imagine having forty wives? God only knows!) They may revere their women, but they keep them under wraps. The men there also wear head dresses like a veil with an eye-slit. There are some very frightening, scary people.

We toured the inside of the empty harem and then went to the adjoining courtyard, where there was a turbaned swami playing a flute to control a trained cobra in a big straw basket. The snake gyrated to the tune the swami was playing. I had read all about this, but it was fascinating to see it in person.

On the same trip, Marie and I went to Casablanca to inspect the Oriental rug area. Everyone there was turbaned and did a lot of bowing and scraping. Looking at me, they must have thought, "Here's a hunky!" Without any discussions, they started peeling back rugs one at a time. After three or four rugs, they uncovered a man sleeping, and we woke him up. He quickly scampered out.

I didn't buy anything that particular day, but when I was living at 381 Middle Street in Portsmouth, I built a three-car garage in the backyard. The lot ran from Middle Street to Merrimac Street, and its lot size gave us room for a swing set and play yard. All my surplus furniture and rugs I had been buying in my travels were stored in the garage.

Years later, another life story started in Morocco—the Billy Dang story.

The King of Morocco decided to build a golf course and bring over a US golf star named Billy Casper to teach Moroccans how to play the game. Casper communicated with the PGA that a group could come to play golf on the king's course and meet him (Casper, not the king). Marie and I agreed to go with a group of around twelve players and were teamed up with two Moroccan gentlemen. One of them was a Vietnamese dentist for the king. After finishing, the fourth gentleman departed, and Marie and I were walking along with "Billy Dang." Billy was a real character. He said he was a member of Vietnamese royalty. We were passing a bus when he said to us, "Could I go and get my wife, Nau, and could she join us to play an additional nine holes?" Of course, being nutty on golf, we agreed. He went to the bus and got this charming lady. We played an enjoyable nine holes and they suggested we all go to dinner; we did and had a great time. They drove us back to our hotel.

A few weeks or months later, the phone rang at our house in Rye and a voice you would never forget came across the line— Billy Dang's. He couldn't pronounce Jim, so I was known as Jeem.

"Jeem, I at Logan International Airport in Boston. Please pick me up." Marie and I drove to Boston, and he stayed with us at our home. He and I played golf almost every day he was with us. He told us about his life: how Nau came from royalty and they were embroiled in Vietnamese society and had escaped from Vietnam. I didn't know they had also brought a pile of money with them. When in Morocco, he found out I was on a bank board, and he came up with his private plan. The plan was for me to introduce him to the president of my bank, which I did. Billy's goal was to "clean" his money, but my bank president wisely told me he would have nothing to do with this transfer of funds.

Billy left, and subsequently, I received a call from a lady from Wichita, Kansas. She asked if she was talking to James Shanley and I said, "Yes."

"Your name was brought to my attention by Billy Dang while we were in Morocco," she said.

Her husband was in some capacity affiliated with the banking industry, and Billy had called her because he wanted to go to Wichita and talk with a banking authority. Obviously his goal again was to transfer large sums of money. I guess it didn't work out, similar to what happened with my bank.

Marie is one-quarter American Cherokee Indian and is a knockout; I'm a short, little redhead. The two of us make an interesting pair. Billy somehow found out that Marie and I had been married. We had honeymooned at the Greenbrier Hotel in White Sulfur Springs, West Virginia, but he invited us to continue our honeymoon in Paris. He met us at Orléans Airport and took us to his condominium in downtown Paris. Being the gentleman he was, he explained that there was every facility imaginable. He kissed Marie goodbye and shook my hand before leaving us for at least a week to roam Paris. There was trouble brewing in France then, so tanks and soldiers were on street corners.

We will always remember this trip. It was eye opening to go to museums and walk the streets. Once or twice during our stay, Billy called to ask if he could come by because he had places to show us. He took us around and introduced us to people who knew their way around. We went not only to lunches and dinners, but truly lovely places. He mentioned he had a ski house in Megève, up in the mountains of France, and we went there to see it.

Billy remembered that I was close to conducting another "Jim Shanley Invitational Golf Tournament" and, lo and behold, he decided unbeknownst to me to attend. He flew to Logan, and my telephone rang again. "Jeem! It's Billy. I want to play in zee golf tournament." My group had grown from twelve to forty-eight men, and all of them enjoyed Billy. He heard I was having an annual winter party at "the red house" on the Piscataqua River (a private male gathering club where my pal Ferris was a member), and he called again. "Jeem! I'm at Logan." I would go and get him and Nau, and they would stay at our house in Rye. We entertained them as he had entertained us and drove them all over New Hampshire.

Italy

Marie and I were on a yacht in Lake Cuomo, Italy, and motored by George Clooney's hillside estate. I am an admirer of this handsome man, who has looks I never had and never will have. I especially appreciated his beard and eventually tried to grow one.

I was sitting at the Palazzo Terranova in Perugia enjoying an evening cocktail while waiting for Marie to get dressed when the man next to me asked if he could join me. I said I would be delighted. He told me he had an art store in London and was hired by the director of the Old Vic Theatre, Kevin Spacey. He was to help Mr. Spacey start an art collection in his home. When Marie came down, the three of us adjourned to the dining room and were soon joined by Kevin, who sat next to me. He introduced himself and told us that his main interest was Shakespeare stories. As usual, Marie ordered exquisite wine and the four of us obviously enjoyed the same.

As the meal progressed and conversation ensued, Mr. Spacey leaned in front of me and addressed Marie with the following statement, "I have been asking your husband specific questions, and he answers each of them with three stories, leaving me confused." (It wasn't the first or last time I'd heard that!) He sat back down, and we proceeded to have a wonderful evening. He and the art dealer invited Marie and me to visit them when next in London, but it never worked out. I've enjoyably followed the career of Kevin Spacey ever since.

Portugal

Off Marie and I went on Air Portugal for a very romantic trip to Portugal. The first place we stayed was Rua De S. Pedro. We toured Lisbon extensively and, typical of me, sampled all of the Portuguese cuisine, watched street artisans at work, and played a lot of golf. It had spectacular restaurants. We toured wineries, went from hotel to hotel, and made new friends everywhere. One of the things we loved was that it was so primitive. Some people still rode around in horse-drawn wagons and caught fresh fish for dinner. What a romantic country.

We visited Portugal on our own for at least two trips. One time in crossing the country by rental car to get to the Spanish border we saw a white stucco mountain village. The next day, we drove back and visited the village. I was entranced in one building where artisans were weaving rugs. I purchased a rug to be shipped to California. The rug eventually arrived at Logan Airport. We sent it to our home in Borrego Springs, C.A. where it is in our living room.

Even today, we would like to go back to Portugal and visit. Porto is one of the few places we missed. I suppose it is where the vineyards produce the grades for "port" wine. Portugese wine is simply great, especially "port," which Winston Churchill drank in books he wrote and in books written about him.

Austria

Marie and I always wanted to go to Austria, so I made arrangements to stay at a prime hotel in Vienna. An elegantly dressed little man, the manager of the hotel, greeted us. He had us follow him and escorted us to our gorgeous bedroom, which included a ballroom size adjacent room. Subsequently, we found out Hitler had once stayed in that same suite.

The manager discovered that Marie had an interest in fine wines and generously offered to take us to the main dining room as well as show us around the hotel. He took us for a tour, and we were treated like royalty. He introduced us to all the various managers of the hotel and pampered us. We had a wonderful time in a beautiful place. It was all "Herr Shanley" and "Frau Shanley." It was obviously a big screw-up that they thought we were people of importance. Over the years, we have had happy correspondence with the manager.

Turks and Caicos

During one trip to Turks and Caicos Islands with Greg and Vicki Whalen, we ate at yet another "Giley's." (There was a "Giley's" in Morocco too—they're everywhere.) Greg and Vicki often call me

"Norman." They have all kinds of monikers for me.

Marie and I went to Turks and Caicos Islands many times. My friend, Albert Muchmore, is a native and to this day, we have a wonderful relationship with him and his wife, Susan. He took me one day on his small motor launch, and while approaching the harbor, he ran out of gasoline. He paddled us into shore, which was an embarrassment I never let him forget.

One time, Albert decided to introduce us to his extended family. By extended, I mean it was a tribe! He assembled us all at a lovely restaurant and proudly introduced Marie and me. He said he would appreciate a few comments from me, and being a person of limited public address (can you imagine?) I told them all kinds of anecdotes about his father and me. In the audience was his son, who had a baby boy of his own. To rib Albert I told him, "The poor child looks just like you!"

In subsequent years, Albert said to me, "I'd like to visit you in the U.S. and want to see certain things, especially on the California coast." He asked for a recommendation on places to stay, so we went to the travel agency. The travel agent asked him where he wanted to go, and he replied, "I haven't the faintest idea. I have my travel agent here with me." He subsequently came to California and met with us at our home.

Albert sent his daughter to England, and she became a "barrister." To this day, Marie and I correspond with her. We hope someday to return.

Haiti

I had been in Haiti on the heavy cruiser in the US Navy and was intimately connected with the island. I painted the picture of Haiti to Marie, and she was entranced with all my travels there. There was a golf course on the island that Marie and I wanted to visit to play. My God, it was magnificent. We stayed on top of the mountain in a fantastic hotel. The country then was ruled by Papa Doc.

By happenchance, we also met Baby Doc. We ended up innocently renting a motor boat with a driver, to go to a remote island because we were always concerned about sewerage. Things were primitive. I wanted to paddle in the ocean but not near the city. It was a good-sized boat for the four of us. Lo and behold, there was another couple on board— Baby Doc and his girlfriend.

Baby Doc and his girlfriend smooched the entire trip; she was endowed, to say the least. I remembered them because there was lots of romance. We went to the remote island, swam, and came back. The experience of roaming around in Haiti was amazing. I was entranced with the art galleries, and I still have the one painting I brought back. We were riding around and I remember going by the Duvalier compound with big walls. The closer we got, guards would pop up over the wall.

We were always roaming around in the mountains; just a pair of tourists. Marie always drove, and one time she was accused of driving through a stop sign. A cop commandeered the car and took us to the local jail. They wouldn't let me go in with Marie, so the cop and I had a verbal altercation on the street. I threatened to go to the American legation in Port-au-Prince. They finally released her, and we continued our sojourn.

South Africa

We had wonderful experiences in South Africa. At one point on this trip, we were sitting with all the other visitors in the hotel dining room. The trip advisor asked who would be interested in going to Soweto (Johannesburg's slum where Nelson Mandela grew up). Marie's hand shot up, and of course, I was going to have to look out for her! We were the only ones that wanted to go, so we hired a personal driver who happened to be the son of a local librarian.

We visited Nelson Mandela's old home, where a lady newspaper reporter standing out front said, "We've never had a white man and woman visit." She regaled us with stories of his birthplace, and the driver then took us to the home of his father, who was in charge of the libraries in Johannesburg. I often corresponded with the father after that, and it was a wonderful experience for both of us.

Marie and I were once on a cliff golfing and saw our two African caddies smirking, so I knew there was something cooking. They teed for us and didn't say a word, just smirked. Marie and I innocently wound down the path to the bottom of the cliff and walked along the edge about ten yards away from a pond of crocodiles. I can see the crocs now! The caddies were in stiches. They weren't used to a crazy white couple.

We wanted the opportunity to take a safari so we went to Mala Mala Game Reserve and Kruger National Park. This was one my favorite trips of all time. I reveled in the whole thing! Two guys with guns escorted us everywhere. We rode around all through the jungle. A friend of mine had been there before, and one of the wild African buffaloes' horns stabbed her. One day, we were riding along and a buffalo flashed his red, angry eyes through the bush toward Marie. She happily escaped uninjured. We were among rhinos, elephants, lions, zebras, giraffes, and leopards. It was a simply fantastic time for both of us.

Borrego Springs, California

Marie and I didn't like the bugs of Florida, so we investigated different locations for a winter home. The two of us were golf nuts, so we traveled to California and found Borrego Springs. Today, it is very interesting because it hasn't grown a great deal. Ted Robinson, the famous golf course architect, was completing the eighteen-hole Rams Hill Country Club and clubhouse. Marie and I found the golf course on a mountainside and purchased the lot from the Realtor John Goss. I was involved in the architectural layout, and I personally enjoyed having the house built because by this time, I had quite a bit of experience with architects and builders. We have enjoyed this home for years.

The town is famous as a habitat for big horn sheep that contend with the local mountain lions. It is also famous as one of the places Cesar Chavez started organizing the United Farm Workers of America Union. The valley used to be filled mainly with grapes, grapefruit, and various other fruit commodities. At the time Chavez was organizing, the DiGeorgio family controlled the entire valley. That name "Borrego Springs" alone still has a lot of emotion for people for this reason.

CHAPTER 13

The Shanley Dust

"I'm a humble gentleman with an ego the size of the Empire State Building."

I want to tell about a few other projects I have been involved with over the years. Throughout my career, I usually worked behind the scenes to get things done. I jokingly call myself the "Black Hand," though in a good way. Marie calls it "the Shanley Dust," stuff that sprinkles down and invisibly covers everything. In a choice between getting credit and getting results, I'll take the results.

The North End

After World War II, the Feds went into a program of urban renewal, a binge of cleaning up communities.

In Portsmouth, the North End was almost all people of Italian decent, an Italian enclave. Growing up, I unfortunately spent little time there—it was a close-knit group. They had Italian food stores and so forth, and they owned their homes. The government had zeroed in on this area by the A&P Supermarket for "urban renewal." The coal yards were there. This is from the Sheraton today to the waterfront, where they're having a battle now over the scrap piles along the Piscataqua River.

In those days, if you had a client and the potential buyer's wanted a house, the FHA and GI loans were available. The client and I would get in my car and drive to Manchester, having prepared in advance to answer any questions. That way, I hoped everything would be in order and result in a sale and eventually a commission. We'd meet the FHA and VA executives at the Manchester office, and since I was there so often, I became friends with all of them. I was selling houses like hot dogs, a skyrocket, and I was up there all the time.

When the Federal Housing Administration set its sights on the North End, I was asked to meet with the people who owned property. I went from house to house and met with each family to negotiate the purchase by the Feds of their homes. The government told me what it wanted to pay, but I still negotiated for the owners with the government. It was right up my alley. I met everyone and negotiated the sale of their property. I was the instrument. It was a golden opportunity for me, and I don't know if the owners would have received the prices they did if not for my negotiating fair sale prices for both parties.

I was a twenty-three-year-old guy just starting out in business, so I was flattered the government picked me. Of course, the amount of money the owners received at that time in their opinion was so large it helped. There's controversy now over what happened to the North End, but I've always kept my happy relations with former school friends and their parents.

Urban renewal didn't turn out well in many places—a lot of cities ended up with demolished family homes followed by high-rise slums. Whatever else might have happened, you can't say that about the North End. Now the well-to-do have started to move there, and we have five-story buildings going up. It's somewhat shameful, but some people call it progress.

Much of how Portsmouth developed was because of our doyenne, Mayor Mary Dondero, who was a client of mine as well. She was the mayor for a long time and was really a power. (The Donderos owned the Portsmouth shop on Congress Street where every kid in Portsmouth wanted to get ice cream.) There was a mixture of people involved, but there's no question that the preservation of the South End—Strawberry Bank—was a capstone of her career. The preservation of South End was, as it is today, essential. My first listing was down there on Marcy Street, and I had an intimate knowledge of the real estate values while involved in minor ways behind the scenes there, too.

Pease Air Force Base

For me, it was a business and personal godsend when the US Air Force came to Pease. The officers were fertile territory. They were living in military housing and mainly moving everyone here from Oklahoma. Naturally, they wanted to bring along their wives and children. By the time James A. Shanley Corporation closed, there were offices in Kennebunk, Kennebunkport, York, Wells, Ogunquit, Kittery, Portsmouth, Hampton, North Hampton, Dover, Durham and Northwood. I had contacts in Massachusetts, but mainly I was New Hampshire and Maine oriented. Again, from the GI loan program and other projects, I knew everybody in the FHA and VA in Manchester, and I was able to work well on behalf of military families buying homes.

The Portsmouth Regional Hospital

Hospital Corporation of America (HCA) had come to an agreement to purchase the Portsmouth Regional Hospital. They hired me to look for sites when they wanted to build a new hospital in Portsmouth. They brought their national real estate agent,

Charlie Martin, to Portsmouth. He met with me several times to discuss what HCA required in a site. They flew him in from their corporate office, and he talked to me about how they negotiated the purchase of the original Portsmouth Hospital on Junkins Avenue. It was an old building, a 100-plus year old brick place. I went around Portsmouth and chose twelve other potential sites for them to consider for the new hospital to be built on. Charlie came to Pease Airport and picked me up. We subsequently flew around and looked at all the sites in a glass-bottomed helicopter, which scared me to death.

Underneath it all, I wanted the Portsmouth Regional Hospital to be where it is today. I thought the ideal place was on Borthwick Avenue on land once belonging to the "Dowager." It was perfect, and that's the truth of the matter. We looked at all the sites from the air, and Charlie was a meticulous and smart man. I enjoyed the repartee because he had looked at real estate all over the United States. I'm a little guy who is now 99% bald, and he was tall enough to lean his elbow on top of my head. They purchased the site, and the hospital was built.

Wheelabrator Technologies Inc.

Michael Dingman was a titan coming to New Hampshire. He was president of Wheelabrator Frye, a technology company. His office called to say they were moving their office to New Hampshire, which was an opportunity for us to search for housing for each individual couple and family.

The Wheelabrator staff wanted us to meet with Mr. and Mrs. Dingman and them at the Ritz Carlton Hotel in Boston. They had tremendous demands. I had to provide transportation for my staff as well as the Dingmans and their staff because they wanted their people to settle in the future area of the company's headquarters. They requested that my staff be formally dressed, with the males in suits and the ladies in gowns. Of course, our saleswomen were delighted, and everyone dressed to the nines for the occasion. We had dinner while the orchestra played. We all danced, and then Mr. Dingman addressed the group.

They built Liberty Lane—their corporate headquarters— in Hampton, New Hampshire, and he became a dynamo here. They were also interested in charities, big time.

Realty Code of Ethics (1973)

In my entire career, my legal education has benefitted me. I can read legal documents, so no one can scam me with the fine print. I can't say no one ever tried, but I can't think of an instance where they succeeded. This was very important in real estate, especially in the '50s—people were underhanded, and crooked deals would go on. For a long time, New Hampshire was the only State in the U.S. that didn't have a real estate license law. All a realtor needed to do was send twenty-five dollars to Concord for a license, and boom, you're in. There were all kinds of shady things that went on, but I didn't tolerate it with my own staff—in 35 years, I only fired two people.

My first opportunity as the President of the New Hampshire Association of Realtors was to attend a National Association of Realtors conference in Las Vegas. Since we were the only state without a licensing requirement, my introduction was pretty embarrassing. I came back and talked to Governor John King. I used my legal background to write the first exam, then inflicted it on my staff. They wanted to kill me! The experience later helped me write the first proposed official state examination.

I wrote New Hampshire's first license law for testing future license applicants and tested it first on my staff. I prepared an exam and they took it. I got it approved and Governor John King appointed me chairman of the New Hampshire Real Estate Commission. I rounded up some friends to form the commission and we set out to clean up the real estate business. The legislation eventually got passed, based largely on our recommendations. The New Hampshire Association of Realtors engaged counsel, and, having written the first exam and inflicted it on my staff, I helped write the first licensing law, which State Representative Thomas Claveau helped move through the legislature. We have improved the law, and agents now have to go at least twice a year for an update review.

WBBX

Two men I'd sold homes to approached me about finding a site for a radio station in Portsmouth, WBBX (now called WMYF). William Gildersleeve and I found a site off Islington Street, and they bought it. We formed a board of directors and met at least once a month. Building a radio station was a great experience.

Church School

Father Robert Griffin was pastor of the Immaculate Conception Catholic Church. He called me one night and said, "Jim, the bishop has abandoned financial responsibility for Catholic schools in New Hampshire. It's up to the parishes now to support the schools, and I don't even know how to balance a checkbook! Do something, Jim, to help. We need to get a school board together."

He said he had nineteen nuns and eight hundred and twenty-five children in St. Patrick's school, and he reminded me it was where I sent my five children and had my own education for nine years. I got a bunch of friends together and people I knew that might be interested in helping. We formed a school board. I inspected the building and brought my plumber, carpenter, electrician, and a whole troop of contractors. I had been involved with all of them, and Dan Regan, Andy Fabrizio and I were partners in Danbury Corp.

Catholic kids from all over went there. It was a fantastic education. The old brick building was divided into the school, the nun's office and the convent, or nunnery. I loved being a student at St. Patrick's.

The contractors and I went through the building from top to bottom. The situation was deplorable—the school was literally falling apart. I was appalled with the kitchen conditions, and the nuns communal bathroom and sleeping quarters were primitive. It was immaculate, but not adequate for nineteen nuns to share.

I got estimates for what was needed for the preliminary restoration of the school and convent; it was almost nine hundred thousand dollars. Henry Berounsky of Ben's Auto Body volunteered to go with me to Manchester to meet with the bishop. A reception priest there wanted to know why we were at the bishop's mansion. The bishop's office was at least twice the size of mine in Portsmouth, and he had a massive desk. It was dark as hell and had all kinds of windows and heavy draperies. I think his name was Gendron. He implied after we made our case, "Who are you to request $894,000 from a bishop?" and then he immediately proceeded to turn us down.

We went back to Portsmouth and I met with my Board. At the following board meeting, the bishop sent an Irish monsignor with a perfect head of hair who towered over me and tried to intimidate the Board. He made a pitch about, "Who are you all to confront the Bishop? Who do you think you are?" He presented his mission statement to the Board and simultaneously without any provocation, they all stood up and clapped at Henry's and my audacity.

After the meeting, I went out in the hall with him and said, "Listen, I'll give you forty-eight hours. Tell the bishop I want the money guaranteed to renovate the school and nunnery. If I don't have the okay in forty-eight hours, I'm going to contact the *Portsmouth Herald* reporters and share with them the safety hazards to the children and nuns."

We got the guaranteed money the next day, and my gang of contractors were off and running with the renovations of St. Patrick's School.

CHAPTER 14

Other Challenges

What I Needed Was a Hole in the Head

There was a scab on my head, so I went to a Boston dermatologist. I was in Florida on vacation when she called to say I had a serious growth and needed to fly back immediately. Marie and I got on a plane and flew to her office in Boston. The biopsy was diagnosed as serious melanoma cancer that needed to be removed surgically. She chose a surgeon at Massachusetts General Hospital (MGH) and made an appointment to remove it. I was introduced to the surgeon and two other doctors, who all concluded that we needed to go forward with the operation to surgically remove the cancer. I agreed.

I arrived on the scheduled date for the operation and the preparatory nurse got me ready for the anesthesiologist, who started the intravenous injection and stayed with me throughout the procedure. Upon being wheeled into the operating room half sedated, I noticed at the end of the table a large, round, paper drawing on the wall. It apparently showed the top of my head with my cancer delineated. I was asked in my condition to confirm by pointing at my head where the cancer was. I obviously pointed to the wrong spot. The procedure was immediately stopped and a nurse went into the waiting room where my wife Marie was sitting. They told her about the confusion and asked if she would agree to be dressed appropriately for entry to the operating room. She was taken to the doctor's scrub room, dressed, and brought into the operating room. She did her best to remember where she was told the cancer was cited. The operation proceeded, and when my dermatologist returned from Paris, she told the surgeon he had operated on the wrong spot. It is my understanding that no photographs of the top of my head were taken, and Mass General now has a rule that no such operations proceed without a photo.

The first operation was clearly unsuccessful, so a second operation was performed. The results were unsatisfactory once again to the dermatologist and surgeon. After the second operation, the hole in my head grew larger. Dr. Theresa Hadlock, a great surgeon at Mass Eye & Ear Hospital adjoining MGH, performed a third operation—I'm told to remove the melanoma cancer and graft skin over the hole taken from my body. After all this horror, physical and emotional, the graft didn't work. I threw in the towel and have kept the hole in my head. My dermatologist and I fight about it all to this day, but I'm the guy with the hole in his head! We have remained professional and personal friends through all these years.

Guinea Pig

After a series of other medical incidents, I ended up as a patient at Hitchcock Hospital at Dartmouth University in Hanover, New Hampshire. Subsequently, my wife and I were invited to a symposium. The principal speaker was Dr. Keith Flaherty from MGH in Boston, who is head of its melanoma cancer department. Fortunately for me, I became his patient, and we bonded immediately. He thought I was a perfect candidate to participate in a protocol for a national project to break the shield of the cancer cell.

He said, "You are the perfect candidate, Mr. Shanley! Here's a forty-page agreement to sign!" I was basically a guinea pig, and I didn't care—most often, people at eighty-four and sickly become despondent and stay in bed. Not me. I signed the contract without reading it and joined seventy-nine volunteers around the United States in the trial of melanoma cancers.

Marie drove me to Boston once a week for fourteen months. Upon arrival, an experimental drug was injected, and I lay on the bed for approximately four hours before going home. At the end of the trial, they asked me to agree to a new drug on top of the other new drug, and they injected that for a couple of weeks. The second drug caused trouble with my liver, though, so they stopped giving it to me. They took immediate action and I got my liver repaired.

One day, Dr. Flaherty took me and Marie to a large room with a double screen TV that showed pictures of my melanoma cancer covering my chest cavity. He showed me on the left screen the cancer I had in my chest, and the right screen showed there had been an approximate 50% reduction in the cancer following the first experimental treatment. We were all naturally overjoyed with its success. After that, an article appeared on the front pages of both the *Wall Street Journal* and the *New York Times* saying this discovery was going to revolutionize melanoma cancer treatment.

Dr. Flaherty has continued my care at MGH, and when the Exeter, New Hampshire, oncology department was basically taken over by MGH, his partner in the melanoma cancer department at MGH (Dr. Panagiotis Fidias) was transferred there. I subsequently met with him, and my file was transferred for the convenience of driving to Exeter rather than to Boston. I have now a screening every ninety days, and the results have shown continual success.

Cancer drug fighting melanoma

Seacoast man undergoes experimental treatment

From the *Portsmouth Herald*, September 1, 2014:
By Elizabeth Dinan

Jim Shanley has a hole on top of his head, the only remaining sign of the metastatic melanoma cancer that afflicted his skin, lungs and liver.

"Cancer is the worst scourge of the world," Shanley said. "But the most deadly cancer, melanoma, now for the first time has a cure."

The 86-year-old New Castle resident said he was cured by weekly infusions of an experimental drug he received as one of a group of "guinea pigs" who participated in Massachusetts General Hospital clinical trials. He said his positive outcome offers hope to all melanoma patients and that he's telling his story about beating cancer "to give people hope for the first time."

His doctor, Keith Flaherty, from Mass General's Cancer Center, said the evidence shows Shanley responded positively to the clinical trial of the drug nivolumab, which has yet to be approved by the Federal Drug Administration. Nivolumab was given to Shanley with the FDA-approved drug Ipilimumab, which the cancer specialist said "is the next wave of immune system therapy."

Ipilimumab was approved by the FDA several years ago, he said, but "was not what anyone would term heroic." About 10 percent of patients treated with the drug responded, he said.

Flaherty's targeted therapy trials are for treating melanoma, which in Shanley's case began as skin cancer on his head and spread to his lungs and liver. Metastatic melanoma, left to its own devices, will kill within months, according to Flaherty.

Shanley said when he was "a little boy" he frequented Wallis Sands Beach, where he would "get fried" in the summer sun, after which his mother would slather him with olive oil. The sun exposure caused skin cancer on his head, he said, so his parents took him to a local dermatologist who "attempted to treat the growing cancers."

"At that time, tanning booths started," he said. "I understand now that we're trying to ban them."

His parents next took him to see a doctor in Boston, where Shanley met "the head of skin cancer department" and began a years-long doctor-patient relationship, he said.

Somewhere along the way, Shanley said, he started using sunscreen "but it was too late."

Flaherty said an Australian study has shown a "modest" effect of melanoma prevention by using sunscreen, but he advocates for covering up and "avoidance" of the sun. Melanoma has only one known cause and that's ultraviolet rays from the sun, he said.

"The more fair the skin, the greater the risk," he warned.

Shanley said he was in Florida earlier this year when he received news that he had metastatic melanoma and he was advised to fly home for further treatment in Boston.

"I was taken almost immediately to the operating room," he said. "I saw a drawing of my head on the wall."

He underwent a couple of cancer removal surgeries, before he was told surgeons would have to cut down to his skull. He said he was also offered the opportunity to participate in clinical trials using what he calls the "revolutionary drug" nivolumab.

Shanley said he agreed, before enthusiastically signing a 24-page consent form without reading it. For months, he said, his wife, Marie, drove him to Boston for weekly injections of the drugs, and he'd lay on a bed for four hours "while they pumped the goo in me." It was exhausting and stressful, he said, but a meeting with oncologists who showed him a map of his body revealed that half his cancer was gone.

"We decided to keep going," he said.

Soon, Shanley said, he was declared cancer free.

"I know that I am," he said. "I've had all kinds of certificates."

He said could have had a skin "flap" to disguise the hole on top of his head, but said at his age, he doesn't care about how the hole looks. His new cancer-free life gives him more time to focus on his charitable giving and extended family, he said.

Flaherty said the drug that helped eradicate Shanley's cancer is not yet widely available for use but will be "in the near future," when it's approved by the FDA.

"Compared to chemotherapy," he said, "it showed a clear benefit."

Flaherty said the new drug has shown a 40 percent likelihood of inducing a positive response, but it has yet to be seen how long the cure will last. Prior clinical trials of other targeted and "personal" therapy drugs Flaherty conducted in 2000 included treatment of patients who remain cancer free 14 years later, he said.

"By all accounts, this is truly a breakthrough," Flaherty said. "There's a sense of general enthusiasm that we think is warranted."

What Success Brings

As a child, I watched my grandfather, father, and uncle come home with their paychecks. My grandmother, mother, and aunt would cash them, and spread the cash on the hall desk that I still have. The women would then divvy it up into the proper desk cubbyhole, always leaving some for church and other charities. My father was an Elk, a group dedicated to charity as well. It's in the blood.

I choose my charities based on my interests. I'm very careful; I have my attorney, my accountant and my wife make sure it is a legit organization—look at their books before you give money. I've been scammed once, and it taught me a lesson a few years ago. If I have any question about a charity that intrigues me, I try financially to help. I now write first for the last financial statement, unless I know personally about a local area charity.

My goal in the community is to center attention on charitable endeavors by local organizations that I have an intimate knowledge of, particularly its board of directors and administrators, and find out where the money goes. Primarily, I give where I'm intimately connected. I actually know some of the board directors. For instance, I know Mayhew and Families First directors in this area—who is running them and where the money goes.

I used to give more widely, but have now picked my six favorite charities and am doing something more focused. For an example, in prominence, my primary charity is Mayhew, the boys' camp on Newfound Lake. Any profits from *A Plum Life* will go to Mayhew. Somebody years ago mentioned the organization, and it intrigued me. I became involved and was invited to the camp at Newfound Lake. Marie and I went there when we were able to and had lunch with the boys. We went to all the activities and saw all the things the counselors taught them.

Another program I was interested in started with a Portsmouth municipal court judge. She told boys who had minor problems that if they wanted to work for my pal Peter Rice (he was a Marine), they'd get a day off their sentences for each day they worked cleaning up the two area forts. She didn't want to send them to reform school.

In the Navy, if there was a USO in port, I would go. I've always had an affection for the USO. My other favorite charities are the Salvation Army, Womenade of Greater Squamscott (founded by my daughter, Mary Jane Keane a/k/a MJ), the Portsmouth Historical Society, Families First in Portsmouth, Doctors without Borders, Mass General Hospital, the Portsmouth Athenaeum, and Madam Ovary (dealing with ovarian cancer and founded by Peter Rice's wife)—they are the big ones. I have a lot of nice memories of what goes on in the communities around here.

The Veterans Count headed by Gregory Whalen is another favorite. It has become a big one with me. Last winter there were wounded veterans with limited food living in homes and apartments without heat. Unbeknownst to me, a couple of generals and an admiral solicited my second employee to head up a program. They have now divided the endeavor into three groups. A group of men and women visit these people during cold winters and discover horrible stories of no heat or plumbing, and on and on. They get the invoices of unpaid bills, etc. and take them to the next group. They raise money to pay them off, while the third group correlates it all. I was invited in May 2014 to a big gathering of people who will get to contribute more money. We men dressed like penguins, and it gave the women a chance to get dressed up too.

Naturally, the Joseph John Shanley Scholarship Fund is near and dear to me. When Joe died suddenly, a few of his buddies and I set up a scholarship fund with the New Hampshire Charitable Foundation. Three of Joe's closest friends came over, and with all this talk about his sudden death, they rekindled talk about his days as an auctioneer. There are people to this day who remember Joe as an auctioneer and say, "I would've liked to have hidden in the back of the room! He was brutal." If Joe saw you and knew you had a few bucks, he'd make you cough it up. I told them we should see what they could raise with all this adulation. They raised $123,000 in less than a week, which I matched. A bunch of friends from out of town made additional contributions without my knowing it. The scholarship is for high school seniors who want to go to college. They have a process that meets every spring, and the children submit a form about why they want to go to college. The students get modest grants, but they get cash to go to school. Joseph's widow serves on the committee. Marie and I went to the first breakfast as sponsored by the Portsmouth Rotary Club. The $250,000 first went to the New Hampshire Charitable Fund. That seed money has now grown from family members and friends.

It's possible to come from a most modest start and make money. Beyond making the money, there's a lot of good you can do with it.

Appendix A: Mental "Blocks"

Sometimes the most interesting moments in a life are those pieces that don't fit in anywhere, that just happen. I've always had the following lifetime method of approach to achieve something: I start the endeavor first with a goal, and then lay out what I call "blocks." I keep building these "blocks" until I achieve my goal. Here are a few more of those from along the way:

—

After years of meeting with me, one of my recently engaged psychiatrists told me, "Ever since you have come here, I ask you a question and you answer it with three stories. Sometimes they are together, but mostly they are individual stories. Eventually, I ask you the question again and I force you to give me a straight answer." He attributed a new word to me, "tangential."

—

My corporate headquarters was at 22–26 Market Square in Portsmouth. I could tell a lot of stories of the history of many buildings in Portsmouth.

—

I shook hands with then-senator John F. Kennedy when I was in law school. He spoke to us and came down the aisle shaking hands with the mob as he was leaving. He was sure a good-looking guy.

———

General Eisenhower is another one of my idols, and probably our last exceptional president.

———

My carpenter is Jeff Andrews, and we have a $200 bet on the 2016 elections. He supports Hillary Clinton. I just haven't found anyone to vote as a Republican yet.

———

When I became ill and started having difficulty walking, my wife, Marie, had an elevator installed in the garage. It has been a Godsend! A defect appeared in the lift one day, and I was trapped in the middle. I'm an aging handicapped, and my housekeeper came to my rescue. She called the company that installed it, and they sent a crew. The foreman said that never in his career had he ever seen such a clean elevator without a speck of dust, especially underneath. Karen Drysdale, my "household administrator," has been with Marie and me for lots of years.

———

From the time I learned the English language, my mother was a soft dictator; all the women in my life have been dictators.

—

One of my most enjoyable evenings with Marie was in Arizona at a nightclub. I was able to get a front-row table to see Dionne Warwick and Burt Bacharach. Dionne was his muse and protégé. I see her now as a gorgeous older woman, and I own so much of her music.

—

I was a patient and obviously a close personal friend of Dr. Harold Hoefle. As his practice prospered, he was Johnny-on-the-spot. When I had a continually stressful family situation, he was my doctor. I would go to him in a stressful condition and he would throw me in his car, drive me to his house, and throw me into his and his wife's bed to give me a rest. We four traveled together and were guests at each other's homes. He was kind and attentive to the very end. His practice was purchased by Charles Pinkerton; I was his first patient and his second was Ferris Bavicchi, my pal and best man at my wedding to Marie.

—

People either like me or tolerate me, and I've always had a phrase for fun: "Trust me, Buffy." I use this for controversial family things or when I don't feel I'm winning an argument.

—

I was always in a whirlwind and happy, but worked 24/7. Thank God for coffee!

—

I was forever making contacts; just like I'm doing with you as you read this. I'll stick to you like a barnacle.

—

Marie and I always loved string green beans, and Café Nostimo in Portsmouth has the tastiest. What also appealed to us were their rolled grape leaves. Several months ago, I took the children and their spouses and we got a big table. I never saw so many clean plates! It was a memorable night—one of those fantastic family nights. There were ten or twelve of us sitting around on chairs and the floor. It was a great memory.

—

My wife has inherited diamonds, which she keeps in a bank vault, but told me one day that she would love to own a real Burmese ruby. I went to a local jeweler, who said he didn't have any such thing, as they are rare. About a year later, the same jeweler called to say Harry Winston of New York City had an authenticated Burmese ruby. They got it to Portsmouth and had it set in gold and diamonds. At that time, it was very expensive. I went over to the Pic N Pay supermarket and got a crummy brown bag. I crumpled it up to wrinkle it more and threw the ruby in the jewelry box and put it in the bag. I took Marie to Rosa's Restaurant in Portsmouth and handed it to her in the middle of lunch. She opened it and started crying. It was a priceless moment.

—

At one time, I owned four homes. Right now I have one in New Hampshire and one in California. I've had a few "mansions," and a "Royal Barry Wills" home. He was a premier architect for new colonial homes who passed away. I recognize his architecture when I drive by very beautiful homes.

———

I have wonderful children, and they often go with me to my doctor appointments. All they want to do is help their father, and vice-versa. I have been very lucky.

———

Integrity and honesty can do wonders. My upbringing taught me it would also do wonders for our society. Children are surrounded by thievery.

———

One of my first salespeople has become a multi-millionaire.

———

A friend of mine whom I admired was a known gambler. He was a successful businessman in Portsmouth, and knew I had developed into an above-average golfer. I would play eighteen holes with him and lots of pals and never cheated. I played sixty years and, as I improved, I would often shoot a thirty-three on the first nine, and my goal was to shoot once in the seventies for eighteen. Occasionally, I would shoot a spectacular front nine, and this was going to be my day. I never once broke the eighty-shot total score. He called one time and invited me to Lawrence, Massachusetts to play golf and then afterwards, go gambling. It was like a movie scene with Mafioso types in the room and wads of hundred dollar bills. I was interested, but I was out of my league and soon stopped losing money, but my pal kept playing. We eventually drove home after quite a day.

—

I remember a wonderful time when my sister Mary Ellen was made May Queen while at Westbrook College in Portland, Maine. She was my father's first daughter, and he was delighted.

—

One of my financial advisors once called a conference between him, me and his private secretary. He and I had a heated discussion about where to place my money. In front of his secretary, he turned to me and said, "You are a Cro-Magnon man." That was the last conversation we ever had, but the secretary and I have kept up luncheons and a friendship. She's got her own stockbroker's license now.

—

I was taken by one of my closest friends over the years, Jim Tarpey, to meet Fayez Sarofim, the famed Egyptian-American investor. His bachelor party had been organized by Jim. At the meeting, I told Fayez I had some money and through Jim, he invited me to his office in Houston to discuss opportunities. On I went to Houston with Marie. He had at least two floors of offices, including one whole floor for his art collection. I'm a fledgling art collector, but nothing like that. I was met by his confidential secretary, Mrs. White, and when we went in, he was smoking a four-inch, tightly-woven cigar. He turned in his swivel chair and greeted me. I said to him out of the blue, "Do you have another one of those?" It was my first cigar. Years later, I would supply superb cigars for the men at each of the 17 Jim Shanley International Golf Tournaments all over New England. Marie and I flew to Houston to meet with Fayez once or twice a year for many of the following years.

—

I never spoke to Warren Buffet but he is a real human being, in my opinion. I became interested in making money and investing, so Marie and I flew to Omaha to listen to his speeches alongside his partner, Charlie Munger. I picked up lots of his approaches to investing. He owned a restaurant in Omaha, and we flew out there twice. In both instances, we went to his favorite restaurant and he would sit at an area table. It was intriguing to me that one of the richest men in the world chose to eat there. He would be surrounded by friends—"the Oracle of Omaha"—and all just chatted away.

—

I once flew into an airport in Mexico and saw a huge jet. I checked into a hotel—the kind of place where they greet you and bring you to another desk to interview you. Bill Gates was sitting in front of me with his wife, Melinda. The four of us ended up walking down the lane to the homes we had rented; mine on a cliff and his next door to the right. One day I saw him walking across my lawn to look down from the cliff to check on their baby and *au pair*. I started for the glass door, but Marie told me to leave him alone. He was always watching his baby, and sometimes his wife would be swimming. I was intrigued by what he would be reading every day. Here I am, hunky Jim from Portsmouth, but I did have some familiarity with French. Only one person in the whole week or ten days walked up to him and said, "Hi." He also made arrangements at the hotel for all his meals to be served in their house. He didn't fraternize.

—

The first night my caregiver Marina "Desimone" Vardiko went to get me a pair of shoes, she found all the shoes and fell on the floor and rolled, roaring laughing. Someone had changed my brown shoelaces to black and the white shoes from white to black and on and on. We had to put all the laces back in all the shoes so they matched.

—

A friend recently said to me, "You were always two steps above contradiction."

—

I have a modest painting collection in California and have always had a taste for pretty good art. You can't travel the world and not appreciate great museums. I would have liked to have been a sculptor and a dozen other things.

—

Democratic Senator Ted Kennedy from Massachusetts had heard about me even though I was a Republican. In a funny way, the Boston Irish always had an affiliation with other Irish who were successful. On one of his political tours, he came to the office at 22-26 Market Square, with his Secret Service agents driving black cars, to meet "the guy," me. He came in and took a tour of the two buildings. We shook hands and conversed, and he left. I saw him go out to his car, and Secret Service men opened it for him. He immediately turned around in the car seat, walked quickly back to me at the door and said, "How in the hell did you ever come to own these buildings?" He meant, "Who the hell are you?"

I explained to him the whole story, and he said "You did all of this without government money?" He was a Democrat!

—

George Mendenhall, one of my closest friends and sometimes golfing partner, founded a major corporation in Hong Kong after being an officer in the service. I envied his well-deserved success and lifestyle, but primarily enjoyed his friendship. We had mutual admiration for each other. It was a crushing blow to me that he was murdered in his garage. George's handyman apparently knocked at the front door and asked his wife for permission to go into the garage to retrieve a tool he had left behind. Some time passed, and she wondered why George hadn't arrived for breakfast. She went into the garage and found him bleeding, called 911 and the neighbors across the street. A manhunt ensued and the assailant was tracked down in a parking lot. He drew a pistol on the police, and they shot and killed him. We at Rams Hill in Borrego Springs were all very saddened by this monstrosity.

—

Marie's interest in food, its preparation, cooking and display became apparent early. She would hostess and put on really spectacular dinner parties at our homes with scrumptious food and a developing interest in wine. I never had to inquire what she had purchased for food and what was coming. She became the equivalent of a sommelier with her interest in the blending of wines in food. With the crazy life I lived, I worked 24/7 and would come home every night to a fantastic meal. I never knew what deliciousness I was going to have! After tasking every conceivable wine, I only became interested in chardonnay. She continued to wonder as the years went on "How could an Irishman have the nose to smell and a tongue to taste?"

—

I once sold a house to the commander of the Naval Prison in Kittery, who had a lovely family. He came to me one day and told me the average age of a prisoner was between nineteen and twenty-three years old. He said they had four naval psychiatrists on staff and asked if I could get together a group of family men who would be interested in helping boys that had been abandoned and had committed crimes in the Navy. Of course, naturally, this piqued my interest. Each of us had to be interviewed by one of the psychiatrists to make sure we were balanced enough to counsel the boys. Once a week for over a year, each of us would buddy up with one of the prisoners. We would use the "Rube

Goldberg" approach to each boy and act as figures of success. It was a very interesting experience. We did this until the program was disbanded.

—

My favorite bumper sticker of all time is: "Behind a rolling ball comes a running child."

—

The Whalens lived on Wibird Street, and young Bob Whalen, a little older, sure gave me an occasional thrashing. In beginning adulthood, we became fast friends. We were avid Republicans, and his nickname was "Rabid." He eventually became an orator and got elected to the governor's council in New Hampshire. I eventually hired his son, Gregory, to work for me.
One day there was banging on my office door, and Bob stood with a big envelope, smiling. In it was a license plate the governor had approved for me: "313." In New Hampshire, when a governor was in power, he could allocate "low number plates" to members of his council to give to friends.

One time I was pulled over on Lafayette Road and a tall New Hampshire state patrolman pulled alongside me. He growled, "With a 313 license plate, you must be a friend of the governor." I told him, yes, I was a friend of the *incumbent* governor. He told me, "If I see 313 speeding again, you will be arrested and brought before a judge."

—

My personal tailor was originally Rheinhold Holton, Sr. He was also a client of mine. He had a farm raising horses. My grandfather's brother was one of the big guys at Rockingham Racetrack, so of course, he knew all the jockeys. I asked my friend, Governor John King, to help me arrange to talk to the Rockingham Racetrack officials about allowing me to have an imitation Kentucky Derby, where I would have one of the tailor's pride and joy horses run in a race. He spoke to the Racing Commission about my idea to have the first New Hampshire Realtors derby race, and I had five hundred Realtors attend. I got a replica of the Kentucky Derby garland of flowers to drape on the winning horse. I don't know if the jockeys purposely threw the race because of us, but the newspaper photo showed me and a fellow realtor hanging onto the reins of the winning horse's neck with the flowers, just like in the Kentucky Derby. Priceless!

—

I learned as a child that multi-generational communities are essential. People need to fight to get this back.

—

A few years ago, I was walking along downtown and saw a friend of mine. He asked, "Why don't you come and join our men's group at the Congregational Church?"

I said, "But I'm Catholic!" He just laughed.

Now my son and stockbroker arrive almost every Thursday to pick me up, and it is very stimulating. Each man gets 10 minutes to talk about whatever he wants (no politics, no religion), and the group consists of doctors, pilots, engineers, lawyers—you name it—brilliant people, lots of them retired. There's even the guy who invented the copy machine. I try not to miss it. Down there I'm like a bum after a beef stew! Across the street from the church is Henry's, where everything is home cooked, and the three of us go over to continue our discussions.

The "Renie Rule" is that anyone can bring up any subject they want, and whoever wants to add an opinion can do so, which usually sets things off. Sometimes the subjects are so esoteric, they leave me. There are, however, some things I know about and have an opinion on. As far as I was concerned, we wasted three weeks talking about a missing Malaysian airplane; I finally told them we should talk about the history of prostitution in Portsmouth, not a missing airplane. Quite a short change in subject ensued.

—

My mother was the receptionist of Dr. Blaisdil, the dentist who lived on South Street. His house is now Edgewood Manor, and he was one of my original thirteen lawn-care customers.

—

I had a lady friend who was a concert violinist. I don't know how she and the President of Johnny Walker Red (the scotch whiskey) became friends, but she married an American from St. Louis whose family had piles of money. I did a great deal of business with her husband. She brought the guy from JWR to New Hampshire to visit my real estate office at 22-26 Market Square on the second floor. It was a one-time meeting, but for her, it was important.

He came in and noticed my office drapes, informing us they were the same color as Johnny Walker Red. After that we went to lunch. I won't say I cultivate people; I always take people to lunch. Part of those drapes are now in my home office.

—

Governor Charles Dale hired me to sell his home, known as the "Governor's Mansion" on Miller Avenue in Portsmouth. I approached a former classmate of mine, Bob Shaines and his wife, and told them the property was available. I took them to see it, as it was a place everyone would love to own. The entranceway, the living room, the dining room, kitchen and adjoining rooms were all spectacular. They loved the place, and the sale went through. In the transaction, I sold their home on Hillside Drive. They later built a spectacular tennis court adjacent to my home at 381 Middle Street, and we would often play against each other. Our childhood friendship obviously grew with our respective professional careers. The home has now become the Governor's House Bed and Breakfast.

—

On my way to my summer cottage on Pleasant Lake in Deerfield after a night of golfing and card playing, I went off the road headlong into a ditch. A New Hampshire state patrolman came along. I crawled out of the car and without any unnecessary chatter, he told me to get in his cruiser. Having asked me where I was headed, I told him I was going to my cottage on Pleasant Lake. He took me home, and I explained to my wife what had happened.

—

My days of drinking alcohol are over—doctor's orders. I am eighty-six years old and, as my friends say, I'm "two steps above contradiction." Occasionally, I have one and "I mean one glass" of chardonnay with dinner.

—

My wife thinks I am a child, and I suppose at times I act like one in performance.

I like the home where I now live over the seven homes I've owned, and this home is my final bivouac. In my mind, it's a mini-*Architectural Digest* home. That's what we have created there, and it's ideal.

When I was a little boy and Christmastime came around, I always wanted an electric train set. Because of my parents' limited financial capabilities, they would walk me around in downtown Portsmouth just before Christmas and look in toy stores. It was probably a forbearer of my future that I often picked out the Monopoly game, one of which I have retained to this day. Every Christmas Eve, when my mother and father rented 269 Wibird, I would hide behind the living room couch knowing that Santa was going to bring me an electric train. I would fall asleep and my father would find me, pick me up, and place me in my bed in my attic room. Obviously, I never received an electric train, and when Joseph was born, I bought him a Lionel Electric Train Set. My first Lionel train set is still with me, as I've kept it boxed throughout every house move. It is now set on a shelf above my new train track, which runs through the created village in the basement of my home in New Castle, New Hampshire. We have ongoing train parties and individual showings for children, with grandparents and parents in attendance.

—

William "Bill" Hannon, was president of the Boston College of Art, and Charles "Charlie" Conn, was originally a student at the college and eventually, as always, they became friends of Marie's and mine. After a while, they decided that I should lecture to the senior class as they went out to meet prospective employers. I did this with enthusiasm and explained to the senior classes what people were really looking for was professionalism in their approach.

—

I became involved with a gentleman named Jesse Ware as his realtor after he married Leslie Whalen (Gregory's sister). He had founded many ventures, but he owned a pile with her of beautiful homes. One day, he called and said, "I really need some help." He flew Leslie and me down to look at an estate he wanted to purchase in Maryland. He subsequently purchased it. When we landed at the airport, we were met by the attorney for this estate. The estate was one of those brick mansions from a movie set. I thought we were in *Gone with the Wind*; and of course the estate salesman was a tall, handsome man with an appearance like Rhett Butler. What I remember most is that when we were flying back, I believe over Teterboro Airport, a jet suddenly crossed directly in front of our plane. Our pilot didn't flinch, but we sure did!

—

I was everywhere, but people didn't recognize me as a politician. I think of myself as the "Shanley Dust," moving things behind the scenes. For instance, if you hired one of my builders to build a house (or whatever) and were going before a zoning board, I'd say to you as your realtor, "I would be delighted to represent you in your endeavor but want you to understand that if I feel when I'm stating the facts in our request that we are going up in smoke, I'll withdraw and come back another day."

—

Who the hell am I? My life is hard to follow. I've been with the king's son in Morocco. I ran the Jim Shanley Invitational Golf Tournament for seventeen years. I've traveled about three-quarters of the world. I'd like to say to someone reading this, you don't have to be a Rockefeller; you can do it, too, Johnny!
I've had a plum life.

Appendix B: Memories from Nancy Beveridge

Nancy Beveridge worked long-term for Jim Shanley and knows him better than most. When asked about her long relationship with Jim, she replied with the following points.

87 Things I remember about Jim Shanley and Shanley Real Estate

(with a little help from my friends)

1. My babies sitting in their baby seats on the desks and looking up at the dome.
2. The training program you had for all the agents, taught by many of your staff.
3. That I heard that everyone stood up and cheered at your wedding when they pronounced you man and wife.
4. That you were the first person I ever knew who paid someone (Don Pearl) to install wallpaper where you had to actually cut the edges of the paper
5. The gifts we got for having most sales, etc. each quarter. One picture of laundry hanging on a line that I got still hangs in my laundry room.
6. Typewriters in the vault
7. Being in Jim's office in March and having him turn on the AC because he was hot.

8. Jim going crazy that people sat on the front steps and ate sandwiches and then Jim went out to try to clean the grease off the granite steps.

9. Betty Ballard and Mickey Allen down in the windowless basement.

10. Typing contracts with carbon paper between copies and having to use a razor blade to correct mistakes.

11. Your kindness to me when I described my troubles with Dan... offering to get him counseling, getting travel brochures so we could take a trip, etc.

12. The huge Christmas Tree under the dome and the matching red velvet outfits my daughter Kristi and Joe's daughter Tristan wore to the Christmas party.

13. Tuesday caravan to see new listings.

14. The bus you hired and had us all go on a tour from Seabrook to Kennebunkport getting a tour of the towns.

15. You getting pissed to find the Kittery office closed when Jeanne Spinney went over to Chauncey Creek to help her husband.

16. Patti Poli Bissette managing the York office in the old powder magazine building.

17. Board of Directors meetings when Ferris Bavicchi and Henry Powers came in for lunch .

18. When you found out I was pregnant weeks after hiring me you said "It's been nice knowing you" and I told you I did not plan to stop working... and now I am expecting a grandbaby.

19. Walking through fifty acres of snowy fields in February, eight months pregnant when I sold Carlyn Ring the Raspberry Farm in Hampton Falls. When I came in and stood up near the woodstove to warm up in my polyester dress, the static electricity pulled the dress up to the stove and the front of my

dress melted away. Carlyn still had me take her out to lunch afterwards.

20. Lorraine Wheeler and I taking you to lunch to try to learn the secrets of how to make money in RE as Realtors without hurting our reputations.

21. Representing Phil Serowik building new construction on Raeder Drive in Stratham.

22. The contest where we got Shanley Schillings, I think they were called, for doing things like going on tour, getting a new listing,-a price reduction etc.

23. Letting someone go who did something you did not consider ethical.

24. The Hampton office with Mark Berard, Doug Williams and Janice Lambert.

25. When I said I did not want to manage the Hampton Office, you just closed it and gave me a big office in the front of commercial and told everyone to leave me alone. You said you knew what it was like to feel like a mama bird with all the baby birds chirping for attention.

26. Having no offers on Dan Hughes home when he was Under Secretary of HUD and then getting seven offers in one week.

27. Parking across the street in the small bank lot when I ran in to meet clients and coming out and having had my car towed.

28. The summer party at the Wentworth Coolidge house in Portsmouth.

29. Sandy Domina as office manager and her husband Walter helping in the background.

30. Roseanne Favinger at the front desk...always as calm as can be.

31. The big MLS books that came out every two weeks and were the size of phone books.

32. Gayle Hughes in her mink coat always wanted to hold babies when they came in and would rock them while she talked on the phone with clients.

33. Calling us all in for a meeting on December 29 and telling us you were closing the office on January 1, and you and Marie would take care of anyone who wanted to change agencies.

34. Telling us we could take all of our listings and go wherever we wanted to.

35. You going to Pritikin Center (I think it was) to learn to eat and get healthy. I actually went to the Florida one after breaking both legs and not exercising to get back in shape.

36. Joe Shanley chasing my little girls around the office and telling him he would throw them in the soup pot as they hid under the desks.

37. Your friendship with Joycelyn Caulfield where you talked about how you ran your businesses and how you respected each other but were similar only in ethics and values, not style.

38. Stories of you starting out showing houses with four or more kids in tow in the early days.

39. A tour of the little house on Merrimac Street that you once had as your Portsmouth office

40. Door-knocking around the listing of your home on Washington Road and actually picking up a buyer who bought the home from me.

41. How you loved us to hold housewarming parties for our buyers.

42. The awesome Christmas party when you took all of us and our spouses to Boston to stay at the Westin Hotel overnight.

43. The day of the walkthrough for a-closing on a home on Wibird street, Patti Bessette and I got there to find nothing was moved out yet. The buyer said he would not close if there was anything left in the house. The owners-said there was

nothing they could do because auctioneer never came to get
stuff. With Dan's help, the three of us emptied everything out
of the house in one day.-We were younger then.

44. The *S* logo of two houses on top of each other.

45. The gambling party at the office with black jack tables and
    then an auction where we could bid on items we wanted.
    I still have a coat rack from that night that I bought at the
    auction.

46. Being thrilled that I was able to find a buyer for your
    Washington Road home who was totally OK with closing and
    letting you stay in the house rent free for a week after closing.-

47. Mary Jane as manager of the Portsmouth Office.

48. James taking photos of all of us for a series of ads called "I
    would like you to meet..."

49. Starting when interest rates were 13 % and then seeing them
    go to 21%. And now they complain that the rate is over 4%.

50. Owner second mortgages to make deals work at high interest
    rates.

51. My first sale to my brother for $13,500—a mobile home in
    Mobile Manor, Kittery.

52. Having a bottle of champagne in my desk when I became
    pregnant, which was given to the first person to ask me if I
    were pregnant. Joseph won the champagne, but Cindy was
    pregnant at the same time so he had an unfair advantage.

53. One of my first sales on Post Road where the buyers brought
    two large German shepherds into my car on a hot day and
    they drooled down my neck.

54. When selling a house to someone on Griffin Rd-under the
    flight pattern, with Rt 33 in the front yard and railroad tracks
    in the back yard the wife says to me, "You believe what my
    husband likes best about-this house...the location. He thinks

there is nothing better than sitting on the deck and watching the planes, trains and automobiles go by."

55. Dan Beveridge started a part time business called Property Management Services to put up signs and do other small jobs like put numbers up on condo projects before the term PMS had the connotation it does today.

56. One of my first closings on McDonough Street for $31,500 was to a couple who filed for divorce before the closing and I ended up keeping the deal together with just the wife buying the house.

57. The condos you built on Islington Street which were ahead of their time in terms of their proximity to downtown Portsmouth.

58. Jerry Weiss doing the old Whipple School over into condominiums and Shanley RE marketing the whole building.

59. The annual trip to the dermatologist to burn the sunspots off the top of your pale scalp.

60. I remember telling the officer of a local bank that the house across the street from him (corner of Grove and Central in Rye) was on the market for $250,000—can you believe that, a quarter of a million dollars!

61. How you would not hire anyone from Marple because you said they had been "Marpleized."

62. Judy Tracey remembers when you brought her a brass doorknocker engraved with Tracey when her house had the major fire.

63. In the early days, Mary Williams remembers telling her agents that the Shanley agents were their only true competition and how she came over to meet with you to get to know you as you were so respected.

64. Judy Tracey remembers putting a Shanley for sale sign in-Joycelyn's yard and a Caulfield for sale in your yard for

Halloween and you calling to tell her to get that GD sign off your lawn.

65. I remember when I sold your home on Washington Rd that you told me you had not had the septic pumped in over twenty years because it was not broken.

66. I remember leading some of the new hire training classes in the upstairs conference room in Portsmouth.

67. When the Shanley signs changed from brown to a unique shade of plum.

68. I remember the longevity Shanley S jewelry. I got to a pin with an *S* with one diamond chip in it which I think was for ten years.

69. When you asked me to decorate the Hampton office you let me hire a friend who loved to shop to go select lamps, etc. When she delivered some items to my house one day for approval, the neighbors' dog bit her toddler son on the face-and ripped it open and we had to take him to the hospital.

70. I remember the slogan "Your Best Move," which Lorraine Wheeler later used as her email address.

71. I remember stories of the delays to develop the land for Portsmouth Hospital because of a little bird-habitat , if I recall correctly.

72. My brother giving me my start in real estate by buying a fully furnished mobile home in Mobile Manor in Kittery as his first home. He still has the lobster trap coffee table from that purchase.

73. John and Kathy Walker purchasing two rental properties on Brewster Street in Portsmouth. It was a tough neck of the woods in those days. They should have held on to them.

74. Connie Dolben handling the-rental department.

75. Vickie Jenkinson and Louise Duprey who I think did marketing for the company.

76. How flattered I was when you hired me to sell your home on Washington Road when you had 6 licenses in ME, NH and MA between you two and knew every Realtor in the area. You said at the time I was the only one you could both agree on because I paid attention to legal details like Marie wanted and worked on marketing like Jim wanted.

77. Mr. Shanley summoning me to his office, "Go wash your car, clean it, and call Bill Schuler. He has a new doctor in town who needs to buy a house." (As my old brain is starting to run dry,-I am ending with some memories from Lorraine.)

78. Assigning Vicky and Louise to buying gifts for our quarterly sales contest. Jewelry, etc. They generally knew what I wanted as a gift.

79. Calling out Sue Valentine at the sales meeting as she talked non-stop.

80. Pulling me aside one day and saying, "You see her (Pati Poli), I want you to watch her, walk like her, do what she does, and you'll be successful."

81. Introducing me to some of the area's most respected businesses, i.e., Sise Insurance. Mr. Shanley referred Warren and Patty Wilder to me as buyers. He also gave me many other local business people to work with!

82. Asking me when Skip "would make an honest woman of me."

83. Some of the best holiday parties, at really classy places.

84. One of our Christmas parties held at the Kittery office.

85. Recycling paper from the trash cans in the "vault," where the work stations/typewriters were.

86. Absolutely no eating or drinking at our desks in the dome room.

87. That sad letter of Dec. 29, 1987, Mr. Shanley's retirement, and the office phone ringing off the hook with local brokers calling to solicit all of his agents. Quite a testament to Mr. Shanley's staff, our training, etc. Everyone wanted us!

—

Happy Birthday to a wonderful man who has made a lasting impact on so many people, our industry and the landscape of Portsmouth and beyond.

Appendix C: A List of Life Achievements

- Born an American
- Family of father, mother, grandfather, grandmother, caring uncles and aunts, two wives, five children and three grandchildren
- Raised in a Norman Rockwell neighborhood full of families of mixed nationalities and religions
- Catholic education foundation
- Participated in ground-breaking cancer treatment
- Survived metastatic melanoma cancer 2014
- Charitable giving
- Purchased 22–26 Market Square, Portsmouth (historical buildings and first totally corporate headquarters of James A. Shanley Corporation)
- State of Texas, Honorary Texas citizenship, 1965
- Member, Portsmouth Marine Society, 1982
- Found a site for WBBX Radio Station in Portsmouth; one of 10 directors of the station.
- Original stock certificate for founding Strawbery Banke with Dorothy Vaughn
- First President, Seacoast Board of Realtors, 1962

- New Hampshire Realtor of the Year 1965

- President, NH Real Estate Commission 1971

- Member, PHS Football Team 1943–45, Left halfback and scored winning touchdown to beat Dover 14–6

- Member, PHS Baseball Team 1943–45, Second base

- Member, PHS Basketball Team 1943–45, Substitute

- US Navy 1946–48

- Organized original School Board to Refurbish St. Patrick's Parochial School

- Represented PHS Football Team at banner dedication ceremony for 1945 win over Dover

- Graduated from Boston University School of Business Administration, 1949–53

- Graduated from Boston University School of Law, 1953–55

- Met Secretariat, the Kentucky Derby winner

- National Republican Party Award of Merit 2014

- Director, Portsmouth Trust Company, New Hampshire

- Director, BankEast, New Hampshire

- Traveled to many different countries

- My children have all been very attentive to me, and I've been attentive to them.

Appendix D: Pictures of Former Homes

269 Marcy St., my first listing

279 Wibird Street, Portsmouth, my family home

303 Miller Ave., Portsmouth

Fish & Game Road, Greenland, my first home and office

My second family home in Newfields, New Hampshire

381 Middle Street, Portsmouth home and office

Cottage at Pleasant Lake

Rear of cottage at Pleasant Lake

Riverbrook condominium rental

A former home on Washington Road in Rye

Office at 75 Merrimac St.

Corporate headquarters at 22-26 Market Square, Portsmouth, New Hampshire